GET
YOUR
LIFE
BACK

GET YOUR YOUR LIFE BACK

Discover the seven steps
business owners use to create
their One-Life Game Plan™

HARRY J. PLACK

GST
Publishing

Printed in the United States of America

First Printing, 2020

ISBN-13 978-1-7361176-4-4

GST PUBLISHING
UNITED STATES OF AMERICA

To Ashley, Harry, Emily, and Tim

To the years of putting up with Dad and Mom.
From the time you were little children, until the
time you left the house. I appreciate how you
listened to my discussions of how to be more
innovative, how to help people better, how to
do things differently, and how to take clients to
the next level.

Contents

1   Foreword

11   Time Management

77   People

141   Accountability

159   Health and Spirit

181   Sales Process

207   Operational Levers

229   Money

249   Conclusion

251   Bibliography

255   Acknowledgements

Foreword

IF YOU'RE A BUSINESS OWNER, you know the importance of strategic planning. Whether you're currently working with a coach, using a planning model of your own design, or are simply aware of the problems you're experiencing as a result of *not* planning, you know that a strategic plan for your business is critical to your current and ongoing success.

However, many owners fail to recognize that this planning is not enough. Simply put, your current planning process likely only looks at a third of your time. If you're an owner, your work life and your personal life are inextricably intertwined. Whether you like it or not, your business affects your personal life, and your personal life affects your business. Your time is spent switching back and forth between so many different issues, from whether the parking lot is plowed, to your insurance coverage, to whether your employees are fully engaged. Your life extends beyond 9 a.m. to 5 p.m., but most planning systems only look at this third of your day.

It's tempting to put your head in the sand like an ostrich and ignore the sandstorm around you. However, it is better to accept the issues and prepare to tackle them head-on. A system that looks at your entire life—from the nitty-gritty of your business to your personal relationships—will help you better prioritize and delegate.

We think differently.

The One-Life Game Plan™ is our holistic planning model that breaks planning down into seven key components of a business owner's life:

- Time Management

- People

- Accountability

- Health and Spirit

- Sales Process

- Operational Levers

- Money

We work with clients to create customized solutions that work across these seven segments, looking at your whole life—not just the one-third that is most obvious. No matter what model you use, a holistic planning solution can help you run your business better and improve your life.

The One-Life Game Plan™ difference

The One-Life Game Plan™ is something we've developed after 30 years of working with business owners. The purpose of these proprietary planning and coaching services, as well as this book, is to empower owners who want to surge ahead in their personal and professional life. When potential clients are considering joining this program, I often tell them the story of two business owners to illustrate how we make all of these things come together.

Imagine you're driving down Main Street U.S.A. on any given weekday when you make a turn onto Business Park Drive. On the left is Larry's business, and on your right is Will's. They look similar from the outside because they are both successful mid-sized companies. The buildings are relatively new construction, about the same size, and both have attractive signs outside with sharp company logos. They even have about the same number of cars coming and going in the parking lots.

When you take a closer look at the owners, though, they aren't quite the same. For starters, Larry works way too much. He usually works more than 60 hours a week, and that doesn't account for the peak season. His family has not gone on a vacation together for a few years. The last time they did, Larry always took his phone to the beach and pool, constantly answering calls from clients and replying to office emails. In fact, he had to leave his family for a day to run back home and manage a crisis with a major client that his team couldn't handle in his absence.

Larry truly wants to spend more time with his wife. If you asked her, she would say that he's always working and that even when he's physically present, he is preoccupied with work. Larry has the vision of what type of husband and father he wants to be and knows he is falling short due to the demands on his time.

The business is running wild. Sure, it's profitable, but it's never enough. It's hard for him to enjoy the money when he's constantly putting out fires. The business is running him instead of him running the business. In recent years, work has taken a toll on Larry's mental and physical health. He has gained a lot of weight because he's not eating well. A typical lunch consists of a burger, fries, and a soda that he gulps down in the car in between meetings. He knows he isn't healthy and fears undiagnosed health problems because he hasn't been to the doctor in years. Every time he doesn't feel well or has a mysterious pain, a sense of dread—and avoidance—comes over him, causing many sleepless nights. Larry used to have a drink or two after an especially arduous day. Now that he lives in crisis mode, he regularly self-medicates with more than a few drinks.

Larry won't admit it to anyone but himself, but he knows things need to change. He is lost in a cycle that is hard to break by himself. The problem is that he doesn't feel like there is much of a way out. The problem business owners similar to Larry have is that they don't feel like they have a choice. All they see is their own reality. American, entrepreneurial, and business culture have been telling owners for years that what they are experiencing is the norm. The endless days, nonexistent weekends, and sacrifices at the cost of loved ones are what they can expect if they want their business to succeed. They have accepted that owning a business is all-consuming and will eat up all of their time.

It will absolutely consume all they give it, too. As a business coach and an owner myself, I'll admit that running a business takes a lot of time and effort. However, businesses like Larry's will take whatever time the owner gives it—plus another 20 percent. He cannot out-give the business, ever. His job becomes to tame the business. He must set it up so that the business is working for him so that he will have time for all the other things. If he accepts this challenge, then at the end of his life, he will be able to look at things, such as his family and relationships, and be pleased.

Let's contrast Larry's business with the one across the street. Upon a closer look, Will's business and life look vastly different. He works reasonable hours and is happy with his company's profitability. He could always make more money, but he's content. He is able to pay his bills and not run around from one cash-flow crisis to another. This allows Will to take regular vacations without feeling guilty that he is away from the office, and without being tied to his phone. He has a team around him that can take care of whatever comes up when he is gone. Will is able to take afternoons off to make it to all of his children's most important events. He takes care of himself, and his family is thriving. He feels in control of the business, too. He runs the business. It does not run him.

The major difference between these two owners is not how they are managing their money, though that could play a role; it's how they are managing their lives. Not just their careers, but every aspect of their personal lives, too. In this book, you will learn tangible things you can do to make your business more like Will's. The One-Life Game Plan™ is all about moving people from a Larry business to a Will business.

The One-Life Game Plan™ coach

I have had the privilege of working with thousands of business owners over the thirty-plus years I have been in the CPA firm world. As a CPA, I was trained to help people make more money and save on taxes. I believe most business owners want more than that, though, which is why I developed the One-Life Game Plan™. At the end of their lives, people don't reflect on how much time they spent at the office, how much money they made, or how much they saved. Unfortunately, I have worked with too many owners who don't have much else to say or many people to say it to when they are near the end of their lives.

This truth struck me in a painful way when a business owner who I worked with died in the prime of his life. Most people would say he had everything going for him because mainstream culture is materialistic. He had a business that was making money, a big house, a luxury car, and all the trimmings. He had three kids who adored him, too. While his sudden death was a shock, the most painful part was watching his kids grow up without him. Being witness to this made me realize how important it is to take care of ourselves on every level, a concept that anchors the One-Life Game Plan™. If I'm no good to myself, I'm no good for the people around me. If I'm stressed, I'm dying. I'm struggling to survive when I want to thrive. I have to take care of my body and my mind to effectively deal with the challenges that come with owning a business and raising a family.

I want to see people do well and get what's important to them. I've worked with clients who have been in every stage of life, from twenty-somethings to those in their nineties. The One-Life Game Plan™ looks different for everyone in the program. The concepts you'll read about in this book aren't ground-breaking, and maybe you've heard some of these ideas before, but the product I've put together is based on truth and best practices.

I've worked alongside business owners and their families for a long time. I've helped a diverse group of people through a wide variety of situations, and I feel as though I have the equivalent to a degree in counseling. In fact, sometimes, the One-Life Game Plan™ seems like counseling for business owners. I've talked clients through their families falling apart, divorces, and deaths. I take the time to work through these situations with my clients not just because I genuinely care for them, but also because I know from experience as a business owner, it's impossible to separate every aspect of your work and personal life. As much as you may try, you can't be at your best in the office if your personal life is falling apart. Throughout this book, you'll read a lot of my clients' success stories, and you will hear about some mistakes that I coached them through and helped them learn from. My team and I are great at telling people the things they need to hear, and we do it in a nice way. I don't pull punches, though. I invest in working with my clients, and in writing this book, I offer what I believe is best for business owners personally and professionally for the long haul.

My hope is that in the pages to follow, the material will help you make some necessary changes in your life and help your business to grow.

Harry Plack

Maryland

November 2020

CHAPTER 1

Time Management

ONE OF THE BIGGEST BLESSINGS of being a business owner also happens to be one of the biggest curses: the lack of fixed work hours. Making your own schedule is wonderful, but it is a challenge because successful owners don't always want to admit how many hours they work—most probably don't even know.

As an employee, your boundaries are set in place for you and even the possibility of additional overtime pay; as an owner, there are no preset limits or managers to approve overtime. The entrepreneurial personality gets excited by this endless potential—and that is a very good thing.

Business owners need to be up to the challenge in order to be successful. Enthusiasm truly helps owners work longer and harder than they ever thought possible. However, there are problems that are unique to small business owners as a result of this nonstandard work environment. This is one of the first aspects we coach a client on. When an owner is asked how many hours he or she works, they'll often ramble on about how busy they are but can't even come up with a number. When we probe deeper, owners always underestimate how much they work. It's common to discover that they're not home for dinner much, that they spend most Saturdays in the office, and Sunday nights are usually spent on their computers prepping for the week ahead. Without a clearly demarcated line between work and life, business owners face something that I like to call *time creep*.

What is time creep?

Your business is not your boss. It is not something that you can easily get away from—it's always over your shoulder, always watching, always demanding. Your business can take over your life. Slowly (or not so slowly), the business creeps up on you, taking up more and more of your time. Unlike a boss, the business has no boundaries. Therefore, there is no upper limit to what it can demand of you, and your business will take all the time it can squeeze out of you. If you have ever sat on the beach and watched the tide come in, then you are familiar with this idea. Slowly but surely, the water's edge gets further and further up the shore, until it finally soaks the first row of unsuspecting sunbathers. If your business is the ocean, you are sitting in the splash zone—and you might not even be aware of it.

In author and entrepreneur Michael Gerber's book, *The E-Myth Revisited: Why Most Small Businesses Don't Work and What to Do About It*, he writes about owners who have lost control of their schedule. I like to paraphrase it this way: "If your business depends on you, you don't own a business—you have a job. And it's the worst job in the world because you're working for a lunatic!"

> If your business depends on you, you don't own a business—you have a job. And it's the worst job in the world because you're working for a lunatic!

When I started my business, I had a baby at home. I had to get creative, so that time creep didn't take over my life. I kept trying to do everything myself, but then I realized it was worth the added expense to bring someone else on board so I could delegate responsibilities.

You may wake up one morning and realize that you've been putting in seventy-plus hour weeks without noticing. Your spouse may complain that you never have time for him or her. You might miss an important event. You might realize you haven't exercised in weeks. In the list on the following page, you'll see a handful of the ways some business owners realized that time creep had negatively affected them. This is what we call the "moment of truth"—when it becomes impossible to ignore or justify the ways in which time creep has infected your life, and your business has taken over. Take a look and see if you can relate to any of the problems other owners like you have faced.

What's your moment of truth?

- Missed my son's playoff soccer game.

- Had to cancel a vacation I'd been planning for months.

- Fell asleep before date night started.

- Looked at my cell phone bill and noticed I'd called the office twice as much as any other number.

- Realized I was incurring too few billable hours.

- Skipped a longtime friend's surprise 30th birthday party.

- Gained 15 pounds eating lunch in my car driving to client meetings.

- Hired an assistant and realized how much time I'd spent on other things.

- Started procrastinating on my important work by doing "dumb work."

- Missed my granddaughter's school play.

- Haven't been to church in a month because I've been at the office on Sunday mornings.

- Forgot my wife's birthday.

Looking at this list, it is clear that these owners are enduring far more than necessary. The fact is, most owners think that they have to work this way. They don't see the problem and actually view it as normal. They have to be coached that this is the wrong way to look at running a business. I ask them to practice a bit of metacognition when we get to this point in order to step outside of their skin and become aware of their thought processes. After all, you can't read the label when you're inside the pickle jar. When you're drowning in time creep, it's not easy to see the problem; and if you can see the problem, it often takes someone else to help you find the way out. Practicing metacognition, or thinking about your own thinking, helps clients become familiar with the way they plan, think, and learn.

During coaching sessions, I provide owners my "third party" perspective, which allows them to get out of their norm. You can see these problems clearly when looking in from the outside. You might be reading this and thinking, *Well, these people are idiots for letting things get this bad without noticing.* However, when it comes to problems in their own lives, owners often fail to see the warning signs of time creep. Owners tend to justify insane demands on their time (such as those listed) by attributing the problem to a particular short-term inconvenience or project.

For example, "Once I get one more big client, I'll be able to let go" or "Once the Christmas season is over, things will die down." Others might rationalize that they will be able to spend less time in the business once a new employee is trained and independent. No matter what your business is facing, there is always an excuse or reason why you are working more than you know you should.

While there is truth to the idea that there are "busy" periods and there are "lull" periods in any business, there is a problem when the urgency of your peak seasons (whether a Christmas retail crunch, an accounting firms' tax season, or perhaps a hiring and training glut when the May graduates join your firm) never really return to their pre-rush levels.

> No matter what your business is facing, there is always an excuse or reason why you are working more than you know you should.

If the hours stay demanding, things are just going to get worse next year. It is critical to look at this issue with an eye to the long-term effects on both the business and your life. Chalking these issues up to short-term problems means overlooking the bigger picture. Yes, there are short-term demands that will eventually die down, but these will just be replaced by different short-term demands. To see the problem for what it truly is, you have to see how time creep is affecting you—and your business—in the long run.

I'm reminded of another Gerber quote that I repeat to a lot of my coaching clients: "A true business opportunity is the one that an entrepreneur invents to grow him or herself. Not to work in, but to work on."

Andy Stanley, pastor of North Point Church in Georgia and a nationally renowned speaker and author, borrowed from Gerber when he co-authored *7 Practices of Effective Ministry* with Reggie Joiner and Lane Jones. One of his seven practices is called "Work On It," and he writes that you must carve out time in your schedule to reflect on what you are doing, how you're doing it, and why. He says that this helps you notice and celebrate the small victories in the midst of a hectic schedule. What he borrows from Gerber, I borrow from Stanley so that my clients' stay relevant, sane, and effective. It's crucial that successful business owners pause to think about their intentions behind their work so they can prioritize and take a positive step in their battle against time creep.

Inevitably, you will be forced to confront the problem—and, as you can see, this is never a pleasant prospect. Different owners have different standards for how long they work, where they work, and for how they work. Everyone will have their own unique moment of realization, but they all have one thing in common: *The epiphany comes when you should be living your personal life, but you feel stuck in your business-owner role.*

Work-life balance is a well-worn concept for a reason; it is particularly important for business owners. All owners have to deal with time creep, whether their business has one employee or one hundred, or whether their family is a spouse, or a group of siblings, in-laws, nieces, nephews, children, and grandchildren. Regardless of your individual circumstances, you will face this universal issue of business ownership. No matter how unique your niche, no matter how experienced you are, you will face time creep because it is a natural by-product of business ownership.

Some of you might see this moment of truth as an event just around the corner. Perhaps you have already experienced this at least once in your life. Whether you have already hit your limit or not, the potential for time creep to set in is never far for any owner. As soon as you feel you have dealt with time creep successfully, the issues will continue to develop and grow in new ways. Time creep is adaptive; it adjusts and finds new ways to take over your life as quickly as you put up barriers to prevent it. For instance, you might set a personal goal to spend time with each of your grandchildren on their birthdays. You put their birthdays on your work calendar as blocked-off meetings. Naturally, you will feel good about this decision and enjoy spending time with them. You have taken a positive, proactive step toward owning your own time. After a few months go by, though, you might start checking your emails during their birthday parties. You might schedule an appointment that conflicts

> Time creep is adaptive; it adjusts and finds new ways to take over your life as quickly as you put up barriers to prevent it.

with the day's plans. Or you might look at the calendar, see there isn't enough time to do everything you want, and schedule a meeting during the time you set aside to spend with your spouse. As you can see, no matter how well you've thought through your priorities, time creep will find a way to reappear. What is so pernicious about this problem is how insidious it is—time creep never truly goes away, and it requires constant awareness and effort to combat. It takes conscious discipline to regularly deal with incessant time creep.

The technology we have at our fingertips makes self-discipline even more crucial. Smartphones make a lot of tasks easier and allow business owners to be more efficient, but some people have a difficult time putting them down, which can become an unhealthy addiction. If you don't make the conscious decision to turn it off regularly, or at least silence some of your alerts, it can easily turn into time creep. I try to get clients to understand that it's OK not to respond to a text message right away. There are very few types of businesses where anyone is literally at risk of bleeding to death. That's why I tell clients that nobody is going to bleed to death if they don't check their email after 11 p.m. If an owner does feel the need to respond to everything immediately, they are essentially allowing people to have access to them every waking minute of the day. The only emergency here is losing your own personal time.

Time creep can do a lot of damage to your personal life, but you don't have to wait for it to hit your particular pain point to realize where and how it is affecting you and your business. It is possible to create systems and solutions to prevent time creep, but before you can fix the problem, you need to be able to identify the problem. If you do not know the playing field, you do not have a chance of beating time creep.

It's important to be effective and efficient. Most of my clients don't have to be coached on being efficient because that seems to come naturally to successful business owners. A lot of owners are not effective, though.

Consider the highest and best use principle in real estate. If you're going to develop a property for its highest and best use, you're going to build a skyscraper. Owners have to think about getting the highest and best use out of their hours. This starts by setting a goal for the amount of hours you want to work and maximizing them by being purposeful and doing what has the highest impact. If you make a to-do list, you have to prioritize every item, and you have to be OK with not finishing all of them. A lot of times, the best use of your time is something simple, like a phone call to an important customer. The purpose won't always be to generate more business, and that's OK. To put that call to its highest use, you just need to check-in and connect with them. Delegate other responsibilities and provide clients with your time to show them appreciation and love. Now that's something only an owner can do, and it maximizes the impact of your time.

The key to understanding how time creep works is to understand the three primary ways you invest time in your business—the three places time creep sets in most. These represent the playing field for time creep. For business owners, this is through three types of work. When you see these three categories, you'll understand how time creep has access to your entire life—not just your work life.

The Three Types of Work

1 Going to work

This is the type of work that happens at the business. You're in the office or in a meeting with a client. There are two primary questions that we'll ask owners in regard to this area. First, is this productive work? Second, should *you* be doing the work? For now, just keep in mind that this is time spent at the office, time spent with clients, time spent traveling to and from client meetings, etc. Both working on your business and working in your business happen here. This type of work is defined by both the *actions* and the *location*. It is the nitty-gritty of the business; it is doing the actual work.

2 Remote work

Whether you're working from home, working from your car, or at a coffee shop. This is the work you would normally do at the office from a separate location. It can happen during normal business hours, or in the middle of the night. With the power of smartphones, tablets, and laptops, the office can really be anywhere. While these are incredibly useful tools, they can also cause you to underestimate the time spent in your business.

These mobile tools are often used for short bursts of work, such as firing off an email while in line at Starbucks when you remember you need to follow up with your assistant about a scheduling issue, or the time you spend in the morning before work using a remote access service to look over your schedule for the day or week. It could be taking your conference call in your home office or on vacation, or picking up office supplies on a run to Staples.

For both client-facing and internal business issues, owners overlook the time they spend outside the business. To clarify: This type of work is exactly like "going-to-work" work, except it takes place outside the office. The only difference between these two types of work is the *location*—the tasks are exactly the same. Some owners have devised a system where they do certain work off-location and certain work on-location. In these cases, it is still the same category of tasks (even if the tasks themselves are not the same). You're performing tasks that *could* happen at the office, but you are *choosing* to do them in another location.

③ Thinking about the work

The third type of work is unique to owners and is perhaps the most important to understand. This is thinking about work. For most business owners, thinking about the work takes up a vast majority of their time. At any given moment, you have 30 or more items you are thinking about. Everything has to be done, but a large proportion of these items are not that important.

Consider what you think about on a daily basis. You think about managing your team, your credit card company, your lawyer, etc. This can overtake the rest of your world and make it impossible to be present if you allow it to. This type of work is the most prevalent, as well as the most treacherous. It is only providing maximum value for a small handful of the items on the list. In most cases, this mental work is not that valuable—these tasks could (and should) be delegated to someone else, whether by outsourcing, hiring a new employee, or handing the task off to an existing employee.

As you can see, this type of work is very different from the first two types of work. While you may never have thought about this as a type of work, you probably recognize its presence in your life. You might not realize it, but this type of work is equally vital to your business. This type of work is critical to providing direction to your business. Without it, you will quickly find yourself floundering. However, this is also where a great deal of time and effort "creeps" in on your personal life. Even those who are extremely dedicated in their resolve to keep email and other remote work out of their designated "personal" time can easily find themselves distracted when they should be mentally present.

	GOING TO WORK	REMOTE WORK	THINKING ABOUT WORK
LOCATION	At the office or at a meeting with a client.	Anywhere you have access to your tools.	Everywhere
TASKS INVOLVED	Looking at profit and loss statements, reviewing orders, billable hours	Emailing people, conference calls, Looking at profit and loss statements, using remote access.	Thinking about profit and loss statements. Thinking about reviewing orders. Worrying about the business. Worrying about employees. Worrying about clients. Brainstorming new products and services.

Obviously, it is easier for time creep to set in during remote work than going to work, and easier for thinking about work than remote work. There are physical boundaries when going to work, as there are technological boundaries to remote work. But the only boundaries of thinking about work are the 24 hours in a day—and the business won't stop until it has all 24 hours. In other words, there is endless space for the business to creep into your life. There is no part of your life that is inherently or naturally safe from time creep because it exists even in your thought life. To time creep, nothing is sacred. Because of the demands on your time, you are always at risk of being distracted. The first step is acknowledging that this drain on your mental processes actually constitutes work.

These three types of work are the three ways time creep manifests itself in your life. You'll notice that all three types of work are *necessary* to your business. You cannot just cut out one of these types of work. All three are part of the reality of being a business owner. These are just the areas that are susceptible to time creep.

Even if you are aware of time creep and set up preventative boundaries, you can never fully defeat it. For example, faith is an important part of my life, and it comes out in coaching sessions sometimes. I realized time creep was affecting my personal life when someone I trust at church had to be very blunt with me. "You say you put your family first," he said. "But, it's not first when you look at your schedule."

It was as if the Lord was speaking to me, telling me to stop talking about spending more time with my family and actually do it. I had to make a decision right there, stop making excuses, and start prioritizing my wife and kids.

Most people who work too much say they are doing it to build a better life for their family. Now, there may be good intentions and an element to the truth behind that, but in reality, they're pushing off valuable family time to "someday." To be straight forward, "someday" never comes for a lot of those people, only regret. I tell clients battling time creep to take action for their families immediately.

Sometimes it's something simple, like committing to not working on Saturdays.

One time, I had a client who was a great home chef. He got a lot of joy out of being home to cook dinner. The problem was, he was never home for dinner. So, not only was he not getting that family time around the table, he was robbing himself of something he enjoyed.

Right away, I told him to commit to being home for dinner at least three nights a week. He figured out how to make that work. His business never suffered, and all of a sudden, he had that joy back in his life.

Now that it is clear what time creep is (and what areas of your time it affects), we can discuss not just where it is, but why it exists. In the next section, we'll delve deeper into the issue of time creep.

Prioritization and Effectiveness

As a business owner, there is a wide breadth of items for which you are responsible. This manifests itself in a massive to-do list, whether it's on a daily, weekly, or monthly basis. No matter the size of your business, there is a wide swath of projects and items that are ultimately your responsibility. A variety of information is coming in as fast as you can process it—maybe even faster. In a single day, you might be dealing with an insurance adjuster, trying to get reimbursed because lightning struck your building, talking to a key employee having problems at home, looking at monthly profits (that are down), choosing a contractor to remove snow, and providing your customers with the best product possible. Even if you could get to everything on the to-do list, you would find that, at the end of the day, more items appear. The business generates endless problems and issues that need resolution, regardless of how well-managed the employees are, how knowledgeable the owner is about the business's financial status, or how well the product is designed. This break-neck pace is part of the appeal of owning and running a business. The constant demands are a challenge to be overcome. As time passes, you will start to realize that this is a game that cannot be won.

> Even if you could get to everything on your to-do list, you will find that at the end of the day, more items appear.

Business owners often intend to slow down and work less when their company reaches a certain milestone. Sometimes it's something tangible they foresee happening in the near future. Other times it's a far-off goal that isn't clear to anybody. The truth is that it's hard for owners to slow down when their businesses go from startups to successful, developing companies. When you start a company, you take on every task because either you get it done personally or it doesn't get done at all. It takes a long time to work at a fast pace to build the nucleus of a successful company.

If you live in a part of the country where it snows, you'll appreciate this illustration. There are two types of snow: wet snow and dry snow. Wet snow is easy to pack and build with. Dry snow, however, is powder. The first time you grab some to make a snowball, it falls right between your fingers. Think of the dry, powdery snow as your startup company. If you don't get creative, or if you fail to adapt, it will slip right through your fingers, and you are the only person who can do anything to prevent that. You have to work even harder with dry snow and new businesses, to form that nucleus. You work feverishly to pack whatever you can into your hands, and that's the hardest part. Once you get going, though, you can roll it, and it gets bigger and bigger. When the snowball effect starts happening, the type of work you have to do changes. So, when your business starts developing beyond a startup, you have different responsibilities as an owner. You're not responsible for every tiny snowflake anymore. Now, you are in charge of guiding its direction and growth.

No matter how *good* you are, and no matter how good your business is, the to-do list is endless. Like time creep, the to-do list is adaptive. As you cross items off the list, new ones crop up immediately. This is not inherently a bad thing—healthy businesses are growing, which generates fresh problems. The term *growing pains* accurately captures how difficult it can be to handle the new challenges as your business matures. However, this can cause problems for owners, especially when the company is too dependent on them.

Range Problems

Everyone ultimately reports to the owner. Every department is a direct report. You might be thinking, "I only have five direct reports," but you're dealing with accounting, HR, and an extremely broad range of problems. Regardless of your level of involvement in a project, you are the ultimate source of information, guidance, and general problem-solving. To employees, it seems logical to ask you all sorts of questions, simply because you are the final arbiter of everything. The buck stops at your desk. No matter how niche your business may be, you will experience these range problems. The side issues associated with running a business, often administrative in nature, crop up repeatedly and cause a lot of the breadth problems.

The to-do list is adaptive.

Depth problems

Besides this issue of range is the issue of depth. Some of the problems you are dealing with are high level (such as declining profits). Other problems are extremely low level, such as contacting the snow removal company. This is not critical to your business, but it has to be done. If you have not delegated it, it ends up on your desk by default. This is a critical concept to understand: miscellaneous items (the bulk of the to-do list) will always come back to you, the owner, by default. Regardless of whether or not it is logical for you to handle the problem, it becomes your problem. You'll notice that the vast majority of miscellaneous items are low-level items. They are not particularly complex, nor are they so critical. However, they still need to be done.

Why does this happen even in organizations that have good delegation in place already? Because the to-do list is adaptive, just like time creep. There are always additional things for an owner to accomplish. There are so many moving pieces that are constantly changing and owners take on way too many of those responsibilities. Your business is not your boss; it does not have a finite capacity for adding items to your desk. As you solve problems, new issues arise. When you have an adaptive list of items, and you are the problem solver by default, which results in a great deal of unnecessary work added to your plate. In other words, your business owner role is expanded by one item every time you have to deal with a new problem. Even if these are rarely recurring scenarios, the fact that these become your problem means that other, equally irrelevant problems will also become your problem. In One-Life Game Plan™ coaching sessions, we try to get owners the biggest bang for their buck and focus on the biggest problems that are getting in the way of leading happy, healthy lives.

One reason many owners find this to be such a problem is because the behaviors that made them successful during the startup phase become problematic once their businesses mature. In other words: the behavior of a successful starter is different from the behavior of a successful runner. Most business owners know this and have adjusted on many levels. For example, one of the first things most business owners stop doing is sweeping the floors. There are a few items that most owners start delegating fairly quickly, and most manual labor falls into this category. Sure, early on in the business, it made sense to quickly sweep up while you were waiting for a meeting. It kept the business going. But now that is a waste of time—you should spend those five minutes knocking something off the to-do list (again, that pesky adaptive to-do list comes up). You're not sweeping the floors anymore. This is a step in the right direction. What got you here isn't going to get you further. Some people start businesses to replace their salaried income and be their own boss. Maybe cleaning your own office helped you achieve that goal, but it won't get your company to the next level.

When I meet an owner who is in this transition with a developing company, sometimes I have to give them a leadership orientation. Now that your business is growing, you're not just an owner anymore. You're a leader.

This is a critical time in the life of a business, and there are systems you must put in place. Verne Harnish wrote a book on this process called *Scaling Up: How a Few Companies Make It... and Why the Rest Don't*. A major part of this process is about training your people. Leaders have to—or *get* to—decide how every job is done.

Let's think smaller here. Do you like your coffee a certain way? A lot of businesses run on caffeine. Write down the steps for how to make it the way you like so that every employee is capable of making it on their first day.

Now that your business is **growing**, you're not just an owner anymore. You're a *leader*.

Think of your essential business systems this way, too. Put down your key systems on paper and train people how to do them so you can take some responsibilities off your to-do list. Chances are that you have great employees who want to help you, so let them.

Many owners are still doing too much *in* their business, and not enough *on* their business, despite the fact that they have been delegating responsibilities to employees. To see a fully-fleshed out version of this concept, *E-Myth* is a fantastic resource that we recommend to all our clients. Even if you've allotted a specific amount of time, this isn't enough to combat time creep. Something I refer to a lot when discussing time creep is the 20-percent principle: your business takes whatever you give it, plus another 20 percent.

These demands take place in a field without boundaries. It is the combination of an unlimited playing field (the three types of work that we outlined earlier in the chapter) and unlimited demands that make business owners susceptible to time creep. And, according to the 20-percent principle, the more time you give your business, the bigger the playing field gets. Gave 60 hours? The business got 72 hours. We'll go into much more detail on this later.

The question now becomes, how do you prioritize the constantly changing to-do list in your head? How do you combat being responsible for certain tasks by default? It's easy to set boundaries at a single moment at a time, but the next moment, the demands have changed, and you may struggle to regroup. You're constantly juggling. Time is a limited resource, so it often feels like you're shortchanging one area of the business just to cover another. It seems impossible to keep up with the situation.

At its worst, it feels like you're constantly doing damage control in your business—plugging holes, without actually fixing the leak. You make time to call the snowplow by doing payroll earlier, which knocks out your planning time. Because everything is connected, this kind of shuffle is particularly detrimental.

Time is a scarce resource. It's important to know how to categorize your time. Look at the two issues of range and depth to categorize your time. If you have different departments, look at how much time you're spending on each department relative to the others.

Culture, communication, and the to-do list

Managing time is the toughest growing pain for developing businesses, but a lack of a clear company culture is one of the most important things to overcome. Owners must effectively communicate what their company is about. Solely making money is not a reason to have a business. I work with my clients on defining their "why." What are their values? What makes their company different?

The next step is communicating those values and making sure every employee knows them. I tell clients that if they're not talking about company culture to the point that they're sick of it, then they're not talking about it enough. Some companies have a good-intentioned, well-written vision, and mission statements all over their walls, and you see them everywhere; the problem tends to be that you don't hear them.

A lot of owners honestly don't know how to talk about culture.

A lot of owners honestly don't know how to talk about culture. They put values on the wall but are clueless about the next step. These are often the companies where you see employees cutting corners, orders going out wrong, long delays, and poor customer satisfaction. I coach clients that a practical next step is to teach employees what a good day looks like. Sometimes the boss doesn't even know what a good day looks like for every employee because they manage behind a closed door. Does the person working the loading dock know what a good day looks like in their position, or do they just show up to clock in? Teach them your values and what makes your company different. That's how they'll figure out what their "win" looks like, whether it's loading a certain number of boxes or how efficiently the job is done. If an employee is the only person in a certain position and has nobody to compare him or herself to, they still need to know how to do a great job at the company.

Solely making money is *not a reason* to have a business.

It comes down to showing your employees that you appreciate and value them. These are not hollow words. You may think you just sell a product or service, but every business is in the people business.

Oftentimes, leaders don't realize they have to develop people. You need to have a program in place to help employees move up and stay at the company. They must believe in the company and that they are moving ahead. Expressing appreciation is hard at a growing business, but it needs to be a priority. The problem I see a lot is that appreciation is not viewed as an urgent matter. As to-do lists grow longer, leaders don't see it as something that needs much attention. Suddenly, you start losing good employees, though, and it becomes a huge problem. Keeping the right people for a long time is what makes a growing company into a successful company. In the people business, your people are your inventory. They go home every night, and you hope that they'll come back. If you lost an employee that you've trained for a year or two, it's likely going to cost you between $15,000-40,000 to hire and train somebody new. Show your employees appreciation when they are doing a great job and make sure they know there will always be a place for them in the future.

> Oftentimes, leaders don't realize they have to develop people.

Little conversations and compliments from a leader go a long way. As an owner, you throw off a big wake because you are a big deal. Your employees will hold onto the things you say. Use your words wisely, so they have the type of impact you want. This is something that just takes a little time to cross off your to-do list every day that can have a huge impact on the future of your company.

Time Blocking

Now that you understand how to categorize your work time and how your to-do list constantly refreshes, you can start creating systems with the goal of preventing time creep or getting yourself out of the business as much as possible.

We've developed an exercise to help clients with this process. It is simple, it is effective, and it is proven to work. It's called "The One-Life Game Plan™ Time Inventory." The full exercise is only available in coaching sessions, but I'll give you a glimpse of how it works.

The One-Life Game Plan™ Time Inventory

Step 1: Track your time

Write down what you do every 15 minutes. It sounds tedious, but the goal is to create an inventory of all the things that you do. As you read about earlier in this chapter, there are a lot of places during the day when you may think you aren't working, but you are spending time on the business.

While you may have a written to-do list, seeing how you actually spend your time (and, therefore, what's actually on the to-do list in your head) can be quite enlightening. In the following chart you'll see an example of how I time-tracked the first hour of my morning.

TIME	ACTIVITY
6:00-6:15 a.m.	Caught up on my emails.
6:15-6:30 a.m.	Spoke to Cindy about new letterhead.
6:30-6:45 a.m.	Researched potential client at the top of the sales funnel while eating breakfast.
6:45-7:00 a.m.	Created and prioritized to-do list for the day.

This is where the One-Life Game Plan™ substantially differs from most planning models. We look at the *entire* day—not just what you do between 9 a.m. and 5 p.m. The vast majority of planning models focus on the typical workday. However, many owners fail to recognize that this planning is not enough. Simply put, your current planning process likely only looks at a third of your time. If you're an owner, your work life and your personal life are inextricably intertwined. Whether you like it or not, your business affects your personal life, and your personal life affects your business. Your time is spent switching back and forth between so many different issues, from utility bills to your insurance coverage to whether your employees are fully engaged. Your life extends beyond business hours, but most planning systems only look at this third of your day. We believe there is valuable data in the other two-thirds of your day, and we want to help you reclaim that time.

Step 2: Analyze your time

There are two types of activities that you definitively should not be doing. The first is things you don't like. As an employee, doing things you disliked would be expected of you. Even when you had a startup company, getting those distasteful tasks out of the way was a high-priority item. In your personal life, there are things you don't want to do that are good for you. However, as a business owner, you need to fight that mindset. The reality is that there are some items on your to-do list on which you will either procrastinate or do sub par work because you do not want to do them. These are things on which you should not be wasting time.

The second category consists of things that fall into your areas of weakness. For some, this is bookkeeping; for others, it is marketing. You probably already have a sense of what items you struggle within your business—the items that are never done on time or are constantly error-filled. Either hire someone to do it, have someone you've already hired, do it, outsource it, or let it remain undone. For some items, this is going to be really simple. Others will be a bit harder. Start by delegating the things you know others can do well; this will free you up enough to find a solution to the other items on your list. This takes a surprising amount of pressure off you. Giving yourself breathing room is high priority. You can start this process by asking yourself the following questions:

What are the highest-payoff activities you do?

If you had 60 items on your list of things you did during the week, and you identified 25 that someone else should be doing, you would still have 35 items left. Out of your remaining items, put a circle around the three to five highest payoff activities: the activities that, for the least time and effort, provide the best value to you. We refer to these as your "core four."

How can you do more of these core competencies?

Are there other items you can let go of? It can be painful, but you may need to delegate more of those remaining items in order to be able to focus on your core four. Be cognizant of your purpose. Figure out how to group these core four together on your weekly schedule to be more effective. When you are in the zone, at your most focused, you do your best work. It's nearly impossible to get to that place every day. Thus, it's often more feasible to dedicate one or two days per week to be highly present and highly involved, working on your core four.

Dan Sullivan's program, *The Entrepreneur's Guide to Time Management*, was the initial inspiration for our system. One of the best things I've ever done is to develop a system based on his and implemented it in my own life. He advocates putting your days into one of three categories: free days, focus days, and buffer days. Make this your scheduling system. A focus day is when you concentrate your time on the areas where you are most talented that can maximize your business's income. A free day is simple, yet important: rest up so you'll have the energy for next week. Buffer days mean taking care of whatever you need to in order to maximize your time on a focus or free day.

Communicate this to everyone who has access to your calendar or schedule. You might color code the calendar (e. g. free days in red, focus days in green, buffer days in blue), or just create an all-day event each day, so it's labeled. You should be able to see at a glance which of the three types of days it is.

Take more time off

Business owners physically cringe when I suggest this, but taking time off truly is the key to being more effective and seeing results. I push clients to take a minimum of four weeks off every year, and up to ten. Work less and take more free time. It goes against the ethos of the startup of the student, of the employee. The business can handle it if you make some adjustments. In so many aspects of our lives, we are faced with a "more is more" mentality. However, as an owner, it is necessary to streamline. Efficiency is key to every aspect of your business—including your own time. As we have already mentioned, when we talk about work, we are not just talking

Buffer Days

Free Days

Focus Days

PREPARATION

REJUVENATION

PRODUCTIVITY

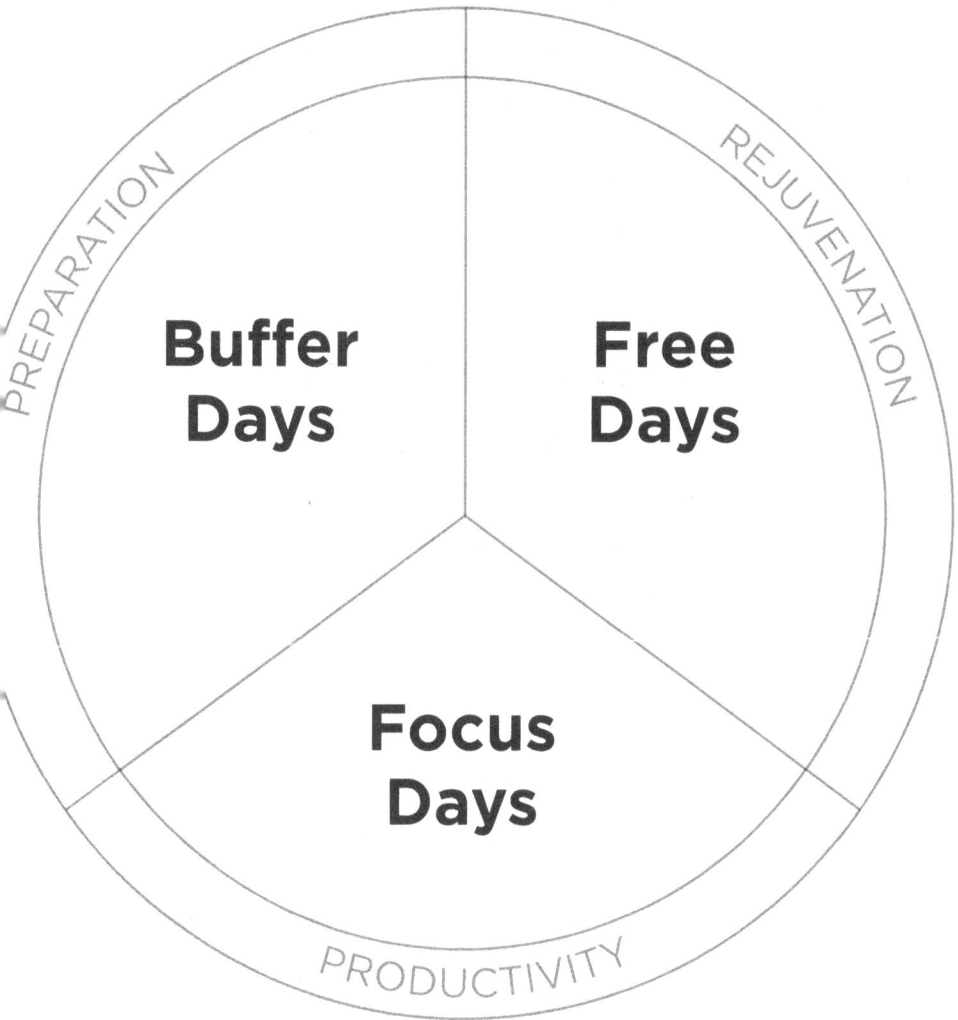

The Entrepreneurial Time
System is a trademark of
the Strategic Coach, Inc.

about the time you spend at the office. We are including those times you identified during the time inventory exercise—every time you engage in one of the three types of work. To increase efficiency, put some boundaries in your world. When I start talking about this, people think I'm crazy because they think "how is taking time off going to be better for the business?" However, it will help you think differently. There are two primary reasons for putting vacations on the calendar.

Plack's 20-percent principle

We already touched on this briefly, and you'll hear it again because it is that important. The first reason to spend less time in your business is what I call the 20-percent principle: *My business will take whatever time I give it, plus 20 percent.*

For example, if you commit to spending 50 hours per week in your business, you will always meet that quota. In a calendar year, there will not be a single week where you

It always takes longer than you think it will.

will not be a single week where you spend less than 50 hours in the office. Just as the average project is susceptible to overruns, the average week will experience overruns, too.

Think about it: when you have a major project, what is one of your primary concerns? Overruns. So what do you do

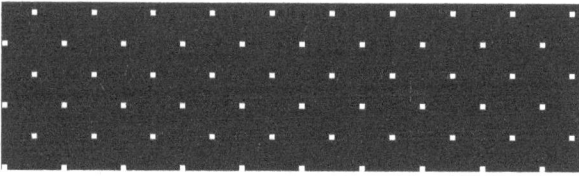

PLUS 20%

YOUR BUSINESS WILL TAKE WHATEVER TIME YOU GIVE IT

PLACK'S 20% PRINCIPLE

to combat this? First, you spend a significant amount of time planning out exactly how much time this project will take. You make an estimate based on how much time you think it will take, plus some extra. Why the extra? Because you know it always takes longer than you think it will. The same thing happens in your business. You think you know how much time it will take—but then one of two things happens. Either tasks take longer, or additional tasks pop up. The to-do list is never fully crossed-off, and you have to be OK with that. Accepting that truth is the only way to get control back.

You have to accept that you will never get it all done. Once you accept this, you can focus on the most important things so you're not killing yourself. If you put more time into the business, you're just feeding the cycle. This ties back to the concept of time creep: the business keeps taking more and more than what you give. The more you give, the more it takes. You have to starve the cycle. It's like the old business adage Parkinson's Law, which says *work expands to fill the time allotted.* If you have a certain amount of time for a task—even something simple—the amount of work will always adjust to match. This usually means the amount of hours will increase, but sometimes you and your staff can get more done in less time.

One of the companies I worked with was a busy medical practice. Everyone on staff put in 20 hours of overtime each week, which inflated payroll quite a bit. When we dug deeper, we didn't think there was reason for any overtime. All we did was put a system in place where employees had

WORK WILL EXPAND

TO FILL THE TIME ALLOTTED

Parkinson's Law

to have overtime approved. After two weeks, overtime went down to zero. The culture at that office considered overtime to be normal, so nobody took notice. Parkinson's Law was in effect at that practice. Their work expanded to the time allotted, so of course they stayed busy the whole time. However, after the new policy started, staff was actually more effective. Like I mentioned before, all we did was require that overtime be approved. We didn't come down hard and say it wasn't allowed or they wouldn't be paid for working longer hours. Still, in a short amount of time, the staff figured out how to take care of their responsibilities during a 40-hour work week.

Constraints Enhance Creativity

Maybe you haven't thought about the relationship between time and energy much, but energy makes me more effective during my time at work. When you're up against deadlines and swimming in your business trying to keep your head above water, it zaps creativity and energy. When you're able to get away, it clears your mind to focus on other things. When you can do that on a regular basis, it helps your spirit, creativity, and energy. It makes you a better owner and the business and better business.

TIME MANAGEMENT

CREATIVE OUTPUT

TIME CONSTRAINT

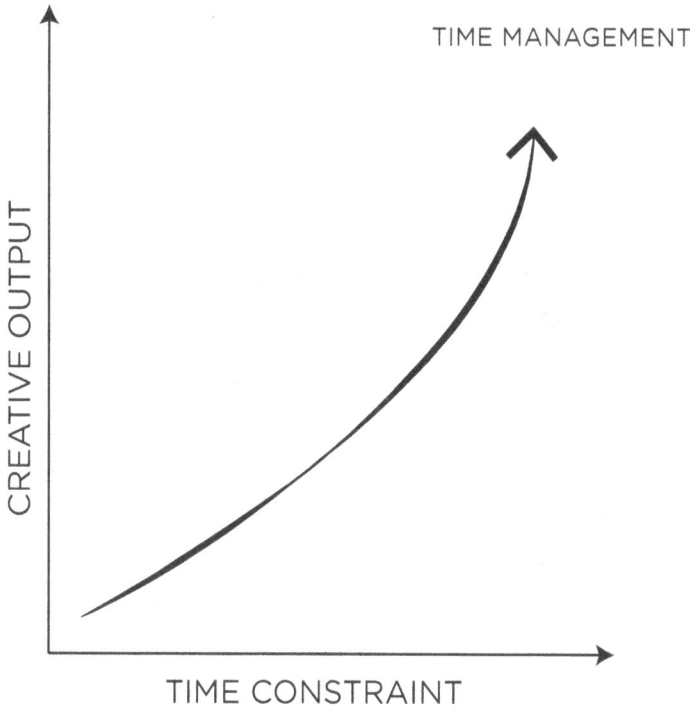

THE GREATER THE TIME CONSTRAINT,
THE GREATER THE CREATIVE OUTPUT.

Limitations force you—and your business—to adapt and improve. Limited marketing budgets lead to guerilla marketing tactics. Limited time forces teams to work better together (we've had a lot of success using the program Basecamp to improve efficiency). Thus, if you limit your business's access to you, you can see these kinds of innovations. Cutting yourself off from the business causes two things to happen that won't happen unless they are forced (necessity truly is the mother of invention). The first positive outcome is heightened efficiency. The second positive outcome is that your business becomes less dependent on you.

I work with several incredible digital agencies. The owners of these businesses are often creatives themselves, and they intuitively understand the benefit of limited resources: limited resources result in innovation. It isn't just creatives who get onboard with this idea, though. Even the most cut and dry owners can grasp the concept. Think back to when you were first starting your business. You had limited capital and limited human resources. Starting from day one, you faced problems that you did not have the answers to. What crazy, innovative, or just plain stupid ideas did those problems force you to come up with? You weren't even thinking about being innovative—you were thinking about solving a problem you didn't have the cash to solve traditionally. Scarcity forces you to find solutions beyond throwing money and time at the problem—in other words, good solutions.

> Limited resources result in innovation

> Scarcity forces you to find solutions beyond throwing money and time at the problem—in other words, good solutions.

Pre-vacation sprint

One example of this concept I often give clients is that of the pre-vacation sprint. Pretend you're leaving with your family for Disney World in three days. You go to work on

Wednesday, excited for your trip, but aware that there are some key tasks that need to get done before you go, as well as tasks that need to be delegated. When you arrive in your office that day, you make a list. Now, isn't that just the best list you've ever put together? It is complete, it is tight. It has all the important items on it. Because you have limited time, you're incredibly effective. You delegate quickly and ruthlessly. You prioritize the things you have to do and make time-effective decisions. You stay on-program because nothing is going to prevent you from taking your kids to the Magic Kingdom. The last three days before vacation, you work three times faster than on an ordinary day, and with minimal mistakes. That is a period of heightened efficiency. What would normally take you 72 hours takes you 24. If you have a limited period in which to work, you're more effective. There is power in that concept.

Additionally, this situation forces your business to operate without you. There have to be systems in place. These systems can either be put in place by you or by your employees in order to keep things running, because there is no other choice. Plain and simple, you won't be there—you are eliminated as one of the possible solutions under the circumstances. The task exists in a vacuum: either you or your employees will do it. This binary choice must be made or circumvented via systems.

> This situation forces your business to operate without you.

A lot will go into planning ahead for that week-long vacation you're about to take. Some of the adjustments you make may be things you want to keep after you get back. For example, you'll realize that there will be checks that have to be signed while you are gone. Typically, you sign the checks daily. When you leave, that system will grind to a halt. What do you do? Maybe you start doing checks once a week. Maybe you let someone else write checks under $10,000. There are a variety of ways to solve the problem; you simply have to find the option that works for your business.

Only four office days per week

Now instead of a vacation, let's pretend that you've set a goal for yourself to only be in the office four days a week. If you're only in four days a week, and you sign checks every day, you have to change the system. You adapt the way you did when you were about to go on vacation; however, instead of going back to the way things used to be (you signing checks daily), you keep using your more efficient system. This can be a breakthrough! When you start tackling problems with the mindset of "how can we fix this problem *without me being involved*," you take that vacation mindset (and with it, the increased efficiency) and use it to improve your everyday operations, freeing up your time dramatically.

You are most effective when you're purposeful. I've seen clients get back from vacation to an office running smoother than before. It makes them learn valuable lessons about what needs to be on their to-do list. For example, owners realize they don't have to be involved with the daily deposit of money because they implemented a system of checks and balances and now somebody else does it.

Another owner thought he always had to be the one responding to requests from a major client. However, when he was on vacation it created a vacuum of responsibilities that had

You are most effective when you're purposeful.

to get done, and trusted employees stepped up and did a great job. When he returned, he realized he could trust his employees with this client and could take this responsibility off his plate. Just because you can do something doesn't mean you should do it. I can empty the recycling can sitting by my desk, and it's a little thing, but it is someone else's job.

In addition, employees know the playing field, enabling them to use all of it. That means when it comes to time management, limitations are the key to freeing you up.

This concept is human-nature. A study done by the American Society of Landscape Architects was conducted to see what effects having a fence around a playground had on a group of preschool children. First, teachers took the children to a playground that did not have a fence during their regularly scheduled recess time. Later, teachers took the same group to a similar playground that had a fence around its border. In the first scenario, the children seemed fearful of leaving the teacher's sight and huddled near her. In the latter scenario with the fence, the students played drastically different and comfortably explored the area within the set boundaries.

The study concluded that given a limitation, children felt safer playing and exploring. When they could not see a visible boundary, they were more reluctant to leave the adult's side. I bring this up to illustrate that when proper boundaries are in place, you free your employees to use all of the field.

So what, who cares?

If the prospect of better work-life balance isn't enough to convince you to make your business run with you in the office less, there is an additional benefit to using this approach. It's pretty simple: It makes your business more valuable (I know I just hooked a big group of readers who were a bit unsure of this whole thing up until now).

When performing a valuation, valuators look at two main indicators. The first is easy to guess: How much cash money does the business throw off to the owner? A business generating $1,000,000 for the owner is more valuable than a business generating $200,000 for the owner. People who come to me looking to build a business that can be sold in the future usually have this measure in mind as a goal. For those who come in with fewer expectations, it is easy to show them how maximizing cash to owner is a critical goal.

However, there is a second measure, one that is less technical. Far fewer owners realize how important this is in valuation. This is the measure of how much time the owner has to be there. To understand how important this is, think of this in terms of a tiebreaker. If you are looking at two businesses, and each throws off a million dollars, how do you choose between the two? Well, if one requires the owner to be there seven minutes per week, and the other business requires 70 hours per week, this decision is a no-brainer. Similarly, compare two versions of your business in the future: Your business in the future, generating $340,000 to the owner, requiring five hours of activity, versus your business in the future, throwing the same cash to the owner, but requiring 50 hours of activity. Once again, this is a no-brainer. The less involvement required on the part of the owner, the more valuable your business will be. Thus, getting out of the business as much as possible is a win-win.

Coordinating your personal and business calendar

As a business owner, you serve in many roles. You wear multiple hats within your business. You also have a variety of "extracurricular" activities, such as serving on a board, volunteering, or other forms of community involvement. Finally, and most importantly, you have multiple roles within your family unit as a husband or wife, a father or mother, a sibling, or a family member. Trying to juggle these three spheres—business, community, and family—can be difficult.

One of the best things I did in my own life was coordinate my business and personal calendar. I shared my business calendar with my wife. This made it much easier for her to anticipate potential conflicts.

My kids are also plugged into my calendar (albeit without editing privileges). If, like me, you have type A children, you will marvel at how much less frustrated the kids are at you—especially if they are middle-school age or older. For avoiding conflict at home, coordinating the personal and business calendar is one of the best things you can do. If you respect your family's time, they will view your business commitments with more respect. They won't be as upset if you have something you can't get out of if you teach them that respecting the meeting time is key. In business, you want to try to avoid rescheduling whenever possible—if you use prioritization in your calendar, make this a top priority (by flagging it, marking it, or turning off editing privileges for this event).

Most family counselors would agree that communication is the biggest problems in a marriage. Taking this simple step will have an immediate impact because it puts you, your spouse, and your children all on the same page. I never hid anything on my business calendar from my family, but I wouldn't always tell them every detail. Now, they know exactly what's going on. I may forget I have a late meeting, for example, and it's not as big of a problem now because my wife can see it on my schedule and anticipate that I won't be home for dinner.

One of the keys to making this work is creating recurring events. My wife, Cathy, and I have a standing Sunday night planning dinner. We tried to make a weekly planning dinner work for years. It wasn't until we realized that we had to make this a recurring event that we started to do this consistently. It is one of the best times we spend together during the week.

At 6 p.m. every Sunday, my calendar says "weekly planning dinner with Cathy." It is a recurring event forever. It's turned into our date night, which is

Create a recurring event for a date night.

something I coach my clients to strive for every week. We don't make it out every single week, but we do 90 percent of the time. On these dates, we have a nice dinner and review items on our personal and business calendars. We usually talk about events two weeks in the future in order to anticipate conflicts. For example, if one of our children has a big recital, I'll coordinate my work schedule so I can attend.

When I advise my clients to commit to date nights every week, some of them throw up a lot of excuses. A common one is not having a babysitter for their children. I push my clients on this, and tell them it's worth paying for a regular babysitter every week, because it will improve communication and their marriages tenfold. I've had clients who also made this weekly meetings work during the day. They'd go on a lunch date while their children were at school. I tell clients who keep pushing back that they're going to fall into the trap of working too many hours to "give a better life to your kids and family," and while that may be true to a certain point, some things aren't worth sacrificing. If you want to be successful in family and business life, you have to take care of the family first.

The way my wife and I plan together works well for us, but it isn't the only way couples can successfully communicate about schedules. You've got to find what works for you. The principle is solid: look at your time in a sense of what's most important and put those things on top. Going through your marriage and not communicating about your schedules is like walking into a river and trying to stand still. The current is naturally going to move you downstream. You have to strain yourself just to stay still. You can't have a successful business and happy family with that mentality. If you just go with the flow, you're going to wind up in the wrong place nine times out of ten. Instead, focus on the most important things.

I tell clients to test me on this concept and they will avoid so many crashes. The type of crash I'm referring to here is when you're getting ready for bed on a Wednesday night and find out it is parents' day at school Thursday morning. Your spouse and children expect you to be there, but you have conflicts on your work schedule. I call this a crash because now you are not only fighting with your spouse, but an important commitment on the calendar has to be thrown overboard, too. If you committed to weekly planning meetings, you would have already had the talk about parents' day and had the time to move things around to make it work. This is a religion you have to find, and there is no time to lose. Collaborating with your spouse will change how you look at your calendar and commitments.

I had a client whose busy schedule had strained his relationship with his teenage son. His son had grown distant, and his grades started slipping. So the dad prioritized his schedule to spend time with his son every week. They would just go out on the driveway and shoot hoops together. This worked better than going out for a meal because they weren't staring at each other across a table. It relaxed both of them and allowed them to let their guards down. Sometimes you get more communication from kids this way because you're not staring at each other and drilling holes in each other's heads. Think about it, that's why kids talk so much when you're riding in the car with them. They don't feel obligated to talk, which relieves pressure. Playing basketball made such a huge difference in my client's father-son relationship that they started doing it almost every night for a little bit. With that relationship headed in the right direction again, it eased a lot of stress, and it freed up his mind to focus on other areas of creativity.

The good news for business owners is that you don't have a boss, so you have more flexibility to move your schedule around to align with family priorities. The down side, though, is that pesky 20-percent principle. The time you spend on your business will expand to what you give it and more. You've got to be disciplined with your priorities. We've discussed how this relates to family, but what about other things? What if you want to work out regularly? Put that on your calendar first, before it fills up with appointments. Block off time for it on Monday, Wednesday, and Friday. It's like the adage "put the big rocks in first." Then other pieces

WHAT **CARGO** IN YOUR LIFE

NEEDS TO BE THROWN

OVER BOARD

of your life can fit, too. If you say things are important, your calendar should reflect that. Little changes make a big impact.

Maximizing your time also increases the value of your effort on activities, such as sitting on the boards of various organizations. If you can commit to that organization a certain amount of time, and being mentally present for that time, you can do far more good and be more productive than you would be if you had to worry about schedule conflicts. As an important person, a doer, and a leader, a lot of people are going to be grabbing at your time. If you're not saying "no" sometimes, your life is out of whack. Business tycoon and philanthropist Warren Buffett even says "really successful people say no to almost everything." Try saying no to things in your life and see how things change.

> Really successful people say no to almost everything.
> - Warren Buffet

A client of mine sat on the board of a charitable organization for a few years and absolutely loved the work. It was an energizing, life-giving, and all around great match for my client and the organization. At some point, though, things flipped. It became draining, but my client had the false concept in his mind that the organization needed him. Could anyone else possibly do as good of a job he had been doing? He didn't think so. However, that fallacy wasn't serving either party. Eventually, he did what was best. The best way he could have served the organization at that point was to step down and allow someone else who wanted to serve take his place on the board.

He knew he had a storm in his life, and he figured out what needed to be thrown overboard. When a storm came up on ancient ships, they had to throw cargo overboard to avoid sinking. The crew started by throwing the least valuable items out to sea first so that they could keep what was most valuable cargo. It's one thing for a crew to determine what has the most value on a ship loaded with gold bars, but it's not as clear when it comes to determining what needs to be thrown overboard from your calendar. What may have made perfect sense and aligned to your priorities a few years ago may not make as much sense now. It's OK to throw something you used to value overboard. Important people tend to overcommit themselves, and it's over a false sense of guilt that they think they are needed. Embracing the idea of saying no, or throwing things overboard, creates freedom. Some things just aren't important enough to hold onto anymore.

Your expiration date

To put the concept morbidly, everyone has an expiration date. When I die, a lot of people will come to my funeral—if it is on a sunny day. If it is rainy, they won't come. Two days later, everyone will forget about the funeral anyway. They will want to know who is going to do my job and handle their accounts. It's freeing when

It's freeing when you understand that you're not holding the world in place.

you understand that you're not holding the world in place. It's not all up to me, and it's not all up to you. One person is just not that important.

If you feel overcommitted, it's crucial that you commit to having focus days, free days, and buffer days, as we discussed previously. The free day concept—blocking off vacations, buffer days, and kids' sports events, etc.—on your business calendar will help you find the "cargo" in your life that needs to be thrown overboard. It helps to have a standard name for these days on your calendar. Business owners already feel like the line between the company and their personal lives is blurred; they may feel reluctant to see business and personal aspects of their lives mixed on the calendar. Of course, I would argue that these people are right. The lines are *already* blurred; but, contrary to their reasoning, the way to establish boundaries is to accept that both business and personal items go on the calendar. Be transparent about this just like I am when "Weekly planning dinner with Cathy" shows up every Sunday night.

If you have already gotten your hands on a copy of Gerber's *E-Myth*, you might recognize what we are doing here. We are creating a system designed to keep the flow of traffic between your life and your business clear. *Throughout the rest of the book, you'll see that we frequently build on concepts established in Gerber's book, and we highly recommend the book to all our clients.*

We want the scheduling system to be able to run on autopilot when needed. Like we said earlier, this not only improves your personal life but also increases the value of your business. If you can get less involved in any area of your business, even scheduling, it will pay off over time.

Taming your email inbox

The email inbox is something that often takes away from owners getting control of their schedule. Now, don't take me wrong. Email is a valuable tool. Using email to communicate details about personal events can be extremely useful and convenient. However, email is also a notorious beast to deal with. When you reach a certain point in your career (and this is pretty early for business owners), it seems like everyone has your contact information—even Nigerian princes.

Having a system in place for email is critical. Knowing what to ignore, what to forward to someone else, and what to answer helps immensely. In addition, know *when* you will check your email.

Know *when* you will check your email.

The problem is each email represents a decision not made, and it's impossible to operate like that.

I'm a big proponent of Inbox Zero. This concept was first introduced by David Allen in his book *Getting Things Done: The Art of Stress-Free Productivity*. The ideas presented in these resources influenced Google on the whole idea of organizing the inbox. The idea is to encourage users to get their inbox down to zero unprocessed emails every day.

Try as I might, I can't get my inbox to zero on a daily basis, though. That's why I coach clients on "Inbox 20." If I can get down to 20 emails that I need to take action on, that's a win. The number is not as important as the bigger issue, though: do you have control over

Do you have control over your email, or are you just checking it all day?

your email, or are you just checking it all day? If your emails pile up all day and you are constantly checking it, that can be a huge time waste. Email is not something that has to consume you. It doesn't even have to be something you have to be solely responsible for, either. It should be delegated. Have an employee taking care of some of those messages, so you aren't getting notifications all day long. When your phone is dinging incessantly, and you're responding to it, it puts you in tactical mode. You won't be able to be in the creative or strategic mindset you need to be as a leader. That's the tyranny of email. It makes people think they are important when they are getting alerts and replying to them all day when really, they are just putting out fires.

I coach clients to delegate their inbox and archive emails that need to be dealt with later. Also, set up a folder for bulk email. Use a filter to catch any message containing the word "unsubscribe." You can always go back to them later, and they don't have to take over your inbox. Nobody wants to be bombarded with 65 newsletters a day. That will scale back your number of emails dramatically and make an inbox with 20 unread messages more manageable.

Personal retreats

We'll cover time off from the health and spirit perspective later on in the book, but right now, I want to talk about the importance of taking time off to plan. In terms of time management, this is key. If you are not proactive in your planning, you will not see all the benefits of these planning tools.

On the highest level, I recommend *One-Life Overnights.* What is a *One-Life Overnight?* Simply put, it is planning while away from all of your obligations. Relationally, there are so many pulls on a business owner on a daily basis (e. g., family, vendors, customers, and employees). The *One-Life Overnight* provides time away to think and write down plans. It is an intensive experience designed to set your trajectory for the next six to 12 months.

Most of the time, these retreats are going to be solo experiences. This is important because you need to calm and quiet your brain. Some of my clients bring their spouse if he or she has an interest in the business. Later, you may want to have a similar retreat with your leadership team or a core group of employees.

PURPOSE

While we can all appreciate the idea of some time spent away from it all, you might be asking, "So what?" The key to the *One-Life Overnight* is a defined purpose. The overnight is designed to allow you to think and write— uninterrupted—about your business. You want to define your purpose. This isn't a spa weekend. It is critical to have a clear agenda for the day or two, you're gone, as well as a desired outcome. You want to bake in time to use your imagination, clear your mind, and emerge with a sense of direction that will carry you through the next six to 12 months. What should the game plan look like? It should be high-level, preferably no more than a single page. It can be in a list or paragraph form. If you're particularly artistic, it can use pictures. It can use charts, too. The format is truly up to you. This is a primary document for your own benefit— it encompasses your life with the holistic approach we have been discussing throughout this book. Whatever you choose, it is important that you come away from the weekend with a clear head and a *written* plan.

LOGISTICS

When I introduce this concept, the response is overwhelmingly positive. However, for owners, the only way to do it is if they preplan a year in advance. So the first step to a *One-Life Overnight* is putting it on the calendar. It has to be set in stone. Do not let anyone double-book you. Ideally, you already have a system in place that establishes "do not book" periods or free days; thus, your employees should be ready and able to work around this retreat. However, if you do not have these systems in place, this is a great place to start. Ideally, at least two nights away in a row. It is critical to be able to sleep on the issues and solutions you think about. You need to allot enough time to come back with a game plan for the next quarter.

Some of my clients start small. I've known people to start with just one night away. Others have even booked a hotel room and just spend the day there. I recommend traveling far enough away that canceling your trip would be inconvenient. However, you could stay in your hometown if you make sure there will be no distractions. Ideally, you want to build up to a two- or three-night getaway every quarter. You'll realize this time is so valuable that you may want to schedule even more time away. One of my clients goes on a personal retreat every month for three nights. Another business owner I know is in his nineties and has been going on solo weekend getaways since the 1970s.

Find what works for you, just make sure you're actually getting away from everything that could distract you. No disturbances, no phone, nothing. You'll need to get in the right mindset so you won't be tempted to check your phone. At first, it may be challenging to clear your mind, but it will get easier the more you do this. Leave the day-to-day behind and make sure everyone close to you knows not to disturb you for anything less than an emergency. Most of my clients don't run into emergencies during their retreats, though. Those that do probably aren't empowering their employees enough and will hopefully learn a valuable lesson if they have to pause their trip and return home for something somebody else could have handled.

This will require some planning ahead. If you don't schedule it months in advance, it probably will never happen. When you commit to the idea, put retreat dates on your calendar a year in advance. You may need to move the dates around a little, but at least it will be on the calendar.

PACKING

Before you leave, you need to pack. Think about what you want to take and what you want to accomplish. You will be doing a lot of writing, so a journal is crucial. I always bring large pieces of chart paper to stick on the walls, too. The last thing you want to do is run out of ink, so having enough pens and markers to document your ideas is important. Since you'll be writing about future goals, make sure to bring any prior goals or long-term plans you have already spent time writing. Some of my clients can dig up their goals from the last 10-15 years. These are amazing tools for reflecting on what you've accomplished and the direction you want to head in now.

MATERIALS

This isn't your average business trip. Bring books, audio books, podcasts, or even links with preselected YouTube videos—the kinds of inspirational material you would not make time for on an average day. In fact, one of the reasons I wrote this book is because I hope people will use it as an idea-generating resource during a getaway. Bring an e-reader, headphones, and a Bluetooth speaker. Ensure that you have enough space to work. No matter how drained you are going into this event, you will come away with more notes than you know what to do with, so preparing is crucial. Make sure you have everything stored in the cloud, too. The output is often some of the best you'll have all year. The bottom line is to keep outside influences to a minimum during this trip. For me, this means planning ahead for meals, too. I don't want to come in contact with too many people if I have to order food. Take on the less is more mentality—don't schedule activities. Keep it simple. You might want to establish a time for lunch, or coffee, but block out enough time to do nothing but write down your own thoughts.

TIME CONSTRAINTS

Provide some constraints to maximize your creativity. For example, you might choose to exercise from 9 a.m. to 10 a.m., and from 3 p.m. to 4 p.m. or whatever works for you. Bring exercise clothes and equipment to get those endorphins pumping. This is an important element for me on my overnights. Working out and going on long walks while listening to podcasts often produces some great ideas.

Pushing yourself physically creates space to think deeper and ask "what if?"

FREE WRITING

If you find you need to add more constraints, freewriting is a potential exercise. What is freewriting? It is writing without editing. Set a timer, and write without stopping for a given period of time. 10 minutes is often a good starting point. The key is to not edit—even if you get off-topic, just keep going. It can be a great starting point for a brainstorming session.

I always recommend clients strive to create a game plan for the next quarter. This game plan should wrap in all of the One-Life categories: Time Management, People, Health and Spirit, Sales Process, Operational Levers, Money, and Accountability.

People often ask me what I do and where I go on personal retreats. I hesitate to go into too many details because what works for me may not work for everyone. So keep in mind that there are a lot of ways to get away, clear your mind, and set goals. However, if you were a fly on the wall, you would see that my biggest concern is limiting outside interactions. I start by thinking about my food. Mental health and creativity starts with physical health, so eating well is important. This means spending some extra money sometimes. It also means making myself comfortable. Sometimes I don't sleep well when I'm away from home, so

I need to make sure I pack items such as my pillow and a white noise machine.

I've been going on these trips for a long time. At first I felt people judging me as selfish for leaving my wife home with the kids. However, my family has bought into this just as much as I have. They know it's what gives me energy for my business and for them. I'm taking time and space to be the best version of myself. When I'm dispassionate and drained, I'm no good for me or anyone else.

The fly on the wall during my getaway would also have to move out of the way so it doesn't get covered up by paper. One of the first things I do when I arrive is hang up several large pieces of paper. These are going to catch my ideas during my trip and are the starting point for the goals I will generate. The first batch I'll start with will have the names of my family members at the top. I'll write their names, their age, and my hopes for them in five and 10 years. I don't filter my thoughts. I write everything down that comes to my mind as I am reading or praying throughout the whole trip. Some people want to start by creating documents on a computer to collect these thoughts. I don't want to mess with technology during this part of the process because a computer may take a minute to load after I have an idea and I may forget.

I take another lesson from Dan Sullivan as I brainstorm and maintain a positive focus. Progress, not perfection, is key here. When I make this a habit, I remain upbeat and innovative.

If I need inspiration to get me going, I start by writing down everything I am grateful for with the people in my life. It always makes me think of a verse from a hymn my grandmother always recited to me as a child: "Count your blessings. Name them one by one, and it will surprise you what the Lord has done."

> "Count your blessings. Name them one by one, and it will surprise you what the Lord has done."

My next step is putting up some more paper. I make a piece for each of the following categories: finance, marketing, people, family, and faith. Now I start writing down all the things I want to accomplish in those areas over the next year. Once again, I write everything popping into my brain and coming out of my spirit without filtering anything. The more honest and true I am to writing down my thoughts, the more freeing it feels. I keep these papers up and keep adding to them the whole time I am there. If I'm reading or listening to something and it inspires an idea, I'll write it down. At some point I usually realize that I am out of ideas.

My trips usually last two or three nights. On the last night, I review everything I've written and circle the items that will make the biggest difference or produce the highest payoff. In the end, I wind up with anywhere between one and 20 ideas that become my game plan.

These are the ideas I bring back to my wife and leadership team as soon as I get back. I encourage them to give me their honest feedback. I want them to draw the ideas out of me

GET YOUR LIFE BACK

during these meetings. It helps me develop the specifics of my game plan and gets my team on the same page. I type all of the goals I came up with and record the date for future reference. I also hang up some of the sheets of paper from the retreat on my office wall. I want people to see them on display so I can bring them in on the latest game plan.

Next steps may also include taking your leadership team or core group on a retreat. If you don't have a team like this, consider creating one. All organizations need one. As a leader, you have to multiply yourself. It also helps to have a team that can help implement your game plan and hold your employees accountable. As your company grows, there is not enough time to follow up with everyone.

My trips happen at least quarterly, sometimes monthly. The biggest thing is breaking away. There isn't any magic to my process. If there were, though, it would be from breaking away. Just like the pre-vacation sprint we discussed in chapter three, going away forces you to prioritize so that you can get the break you need.

Why is all of this so hard to do?

While lots of owners are able to see how the habits and systems they have in place are failing, it is extremely difficult for them to make lasting changes. Despite knowledge of the problem, owners often fail to create results that last. In light of this, why is there such a discrepancy between intentions to create a new way of doing business and the real-life actions?

This is due to the fact that time creep is addictive. Results are addictive. Entrepreneurs love the chase; they love the game. Business ownership is an intense emotional journey. Anyone who has done this knows that while the lows are low, the highs are extremely high. You can often see this in your own experiences. Whether you're running a flash-in-the-pan startup or a business you've owned for 40 years, you have experienced the addictive elements of business ownership.

For people who are often highly analytical, very dependent on their ability to think quickly, one of the most enduring roadblocks to change is this fleeting emotional high. Thus, a big part of fixing the problems you identified in your One-Life Game Plan™ Time Inventory is acknowledging that the siren song of being busy is ephemeral.

CHAPTER 2
People

TO START OUR CHAPTER ON PEOPLE, we're going to first talk about family. You might be wondering why. After all, this is a business book, isn't it? We've already discussed how the boundary problems associated with being a business owner affect your personal life. This affects your family relationships, too. Similarly, when your family relationships are suffering from your work, you are less effective and more distracted at the office.

Once again, we find that a holistic approach is necessary for the business owner's sanity and the company's health.

Business owners are some of the most ambitious people I've ever met. Every single one has a story of overcoming obstacles, learning on the fly, and bouncing back from setbacks. Yet this drive does not guarantee success in their personal lives.

Harvard Professor and business consultant Clayton Christensen explains that when his former Harvard classmates came back to visit the college campus, they were often divorced, estranged from their children, etc. In an essay titled "How Will You Measure Your Life?" Christensen wrote:

> *They didn't keep the purpose of their lives front and center as they decided how to spend their time, talents, and energy.*

Business owners have a similar drive and can just as easily fall into the trap of investing in the business at the expense of their personal relationships. Remember, time creep—your time will be funneled into the business *by default* if you do not identify your purpose and priorities.

We've already discussed how your personal and professional lives are closely connected as an owner, which is why the One-Life Game Plan™ incorporates a holistic approach. Similarly, we must take this approach when we are working on the important relationships in our lives. After all, we are business owners and invest a lot of our time building that part of our lives, but we are also spouses, parents, and children. Our families require and deserve our investment, as well. This is why we must be purposeful in planning when it comes to family, too.

Think of your family relationships on the strategic level. What are your goals for those relationships? What kind of spouse do you want to be? What kind of parent do you want to be? It's essential to set goals for this area of your life. You create forward momentum by goal-setting in your business life; these principles can help you in your relationships, as well. Being able to look realistically at where you are now and where you want to be in the future lets you determine if what you're doing now is working. It helps you figure out what it's going to take to get to where you want to be in these key relationships.

This sounds scary sometimes, and many of my clients are reluctant to think about their family relationships in this way. Some business owners may not even know how to set goals for healthy relationships because they are so consumed by work and have built bad habits over the years. It's important to spend coaching sessions drilling down to figure out where the pain exists. I tell clients that they have to be winning at home before rocking it at the office. There is no prescription for this.

> You must be winning at home before rocking it at the office.

I usually start by asking them about their relationship with their spouse and continue with their kids. For example, I had a client whose wife had their first baby while he was taking on a major project at the business. He was overwhelmed at work and at home, stretched thin with sleep, and feeling tension with his wife, who was going through so much physically and emotionally on top of taking care of a newborn.

First, I decided to unpack the sleep situation. He was trying to do what he could to help at night. He changed all the diapers he could, but his wife breastfed, so he couldn't help feed the baby. A lot of his sleep issues revolved around feeling guilty that he couldn't do more. I encouraged him to talk to his wife about these emotions. He didn't want to burden her even more, though, and felt like they never had time to actually talk. The stars never aligned, allowing him and his wife to be awake, alert, and emotionally present at the same time. The baby was quite fussy, his in-laws were there to help a lot, and he and his wife couldn't seem ever to have a private conversation.

When you're in the thick of a situation, it is hard to see a solution when it's right in front of you. All I did was suggest that the in-laws allow him and his wife to get out of the house, even for an hour. This didn't create a miracle right away, but it helped get them away from the spit up, tears, and diapers for enough time to take some deep breaths. They improved communication and asked how he could help his wife more, and it eased some of the built-up tension. Now, he could sleep better, he felt better as a parent, and he had more energy to be more efficient at work.

Spending time with your children

When it comes to spending time with your children, you don't always have to totally push work aside. I've seen owners get creative and bring them to work with them. It provides family time and helps give kids a sense of what the business is all about. When they find out how hard their parents work at what they do, it teaches them the value of work ethic. I encourage clients who can't avoid working on the weekends to bring their children with them on Saturdays. They can help clean up, even if it's just running the vacuum or taking out the trash. Sometimes they make a day of it by going out to breakfast first. It's quality family time.

A lot of goals my clients come up with for their relationships center around time. Family relationships are the ones you hope to sustain for your entire life, so you must nurture them. Unlike any other area of your life, you have to spend time with your family now if you want any hope of meeting your goal of spending time with them later. Confused? It's like a pie-eating contest where the prize is more pie. You spend time with your family and spouse now partly in order to ensure that you will be able to spend time with them in 10 or 20 years.

Even the biggest workaholics have a desire for their families to move forward. Everyone has a family, even if they're dysfunctional. Even if I have a client who is divorced, they still want to have a relationship with

> Even the biggest workaholics have a desire for their families to move forward.

their kids. Even those with a broken family want restoration. I had a client once whose children had grown up and moved out, but his marriage was on the rocks. He spent years neglecting his relationship with his wife and never wanted to be home. This made being at work more appealing, but he couldn't be effective because issues with his wife clouded his mind and everything he did in the business. As we talked through the situation, he discovered it wasn't that he didn't want to spend time with his wife. He just wanted more harmony. He didn't want to feel like he was in the wrong all the time when he was at home.

That's why setting goals for your family is so important— because it's universal. I know it's going to help every single one of my clients in the long-run, at home, and at work. Think of your future goals. Where do you want your key relationships to be in 10 years? Are there relationships missing in your life? Be proactive about finding a partner if that is a priority for you.

I ask a lot of my clients what kind of parent they want to be. They usually start with a generic response, such as "good" or "loving." It takes more digging on my end and willingness to share on theirs to get more of a response. Is it important to be there for your kids' big moments? That's usually a "yes." What about the small things? What are you comfortable missing? Don't be too hard on yourself, though, because every parent misses some things. Think back to what you read about merging your business and personal calendars. You can choose what is less important and miss that, instead. Or, you can let the calendar choose for you and potentially end up missing some priceless moments.

This is why I call it the One-Life Game Plan™. You've only got one life, so don't waste it.

Prioritization

Once you've determined your priorities, the next logical question is apparent and should sound familiar: Does your schedule reflect your priorities?

Think back to the One-Life Time Inventory we encouraged you to start in chapter one. This was the activity where you recorded what you were doing every 15 minutes. If you have not started logging your time this way, prepare to be enlightened. This time, we're looking to identify the times in the day you spend on family and relationships. It could be 15 minutes spent over breakfast or 15 minutes in front of a television screen. Maybe it's a phone call or a text conversation. No matter what form this takes, record the portion of your day that you spend connecting with your loved ones.

When you're done, spend time analyzing your "data" to make sure that how you spend time with your family reflects your priorities. If not, why not? What does it indicate your priorities really are? Here are some more helpful questions that may help you in this exercise.

Does your schedule reflect your priorities?

Questions to help you prioritize

- When does this time take place throughout your day?

- If you track your time for a whole week, would you see different trends on different days?

- Is your family time lacking? Where is there time to maximize it?

- Is family time squeezed in between other "bigger or more important" items?

On the tactical level, you have to create time for your family. It's your call on how you accomplish this.

I start a lot of coaching sessions by asking clients to use my "Thrive-o-meter" to rate how they are doing on a scale from 1-10. "10" means they are thriving. "1" means they're doing horrible at that moment. I use that information to judge where they are starting out of the chute. Then, we dig into what needs to change in order for them to thrive.

I worked with two men once who were married to each other and married to the business they started together. Sometimes I would work with them individually, but the three of us were working together during this particular session, and it was obvious they were low on the "Thrive-o-meter." When we drilled down into the issues, we discovered that there were two things that were really important to them but that they hadn't had time for in a while.

WHERE ARE YOU ON YOUR THRIVE-O-METER?

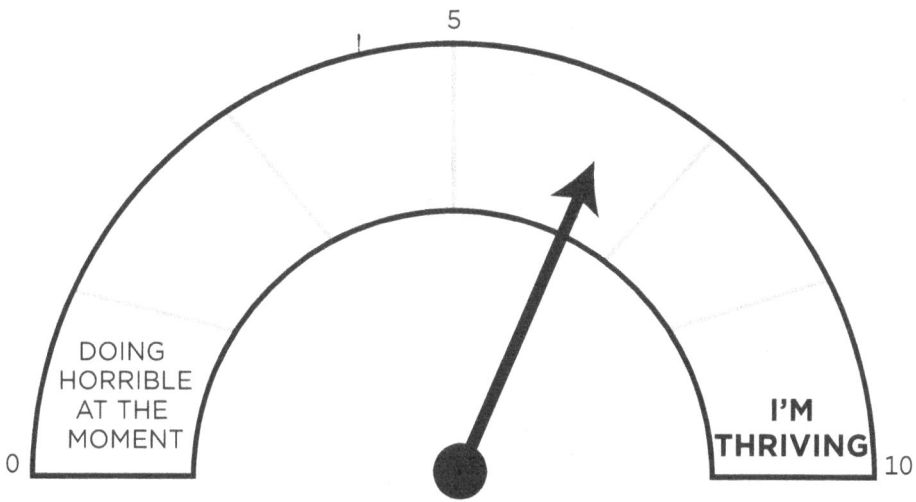

5

DOING
HORRIBLE
AT THE
MOMENT

I'M
THRIVING

0

10

THRIVE-O-METER

WHAT WOULD NEED TO CHANGE IN ORDER FOR YOU TO THRIVE?

First, was focusing on their fitness. They were really into CrossFit and used to maintaining a high level of physical condition. Sometimes they would even work out three times a day. Recently, they hadn't been able to get to the gym. They were feeling out of shape mentally and physically and felt unhealthy overall.

The second thing that was really important to them was traveling. It had been a passion that they just didn't have time for during that season of their lives. They let their hectic schedule cloud their outlook. It bothered them that they didn't even see the potential for planning a vacation for the next year.

Whether you're talking to a professional coach, a counselor, a trusted friend—it doesn't matter who it is—it matters that you talk through your feelings with someone. I was able to call them out on their schedule, not matching their priorities. I challenged them to get back to the gym. They couldn't get there three times a day, but could they get there three times a week? Once they started working out again, it was a lynchpin activity. Everything else concerning their health started to fall into place. They went back to counseling together. They saw their doctors for the first time in years.

I also challenged them on traveling. First, I told them it was important to get away, go anywhere, even for a short amount of time. Taking weekend trips started helping them prioritize their schedules, let certain tasks go, and delegate work that couldn't be let go. Next, I advised them

It matters
that you
**talk through
your feelings**
with someone.

to schedule a big trip—for two years in the future. Pick an exotic destination or somewhere you've always wanted to go. Book it. Put it on the calendar. Establishing these priorities in their schedule didn't rob them of money or run their business into the ground. It gave them their lives back, which gave them more energy and passion for enjoying what they did inside and outside of work.

Mining for details

I worked with another couple who ran a business together. They were both working 60-plus hour weeks and thought making any sort of change to their lives was unimaginable. Sure, spending a day taking care of their grandchildren sounded nice, but they were so bogged down with the tactical side of their company that they could only take care of what was in front of them. How could they clear a whole day? The advice I gave them was similar to what I told the previous couple who wanted to travel, though on a smaller scale. Pick a day. Then, give me a list of the most frustrating tasks you have to get done on that day. Those are the lowest payoff items. For this couple, they had a $60-million company, and one of them still took deposits to the bank every day. The guy still even insisted on doing a lot of the accounting work because he had been burned in the past and was still dealing with control issues in the aftermath. I finally got him to realize that these were unrealistic fears to hold onto and that it was totally within his power to hire a controller or accountant. He had fallen into a bad habit of doing the books himself, didn't mind it, and was actually pretty good at it. However, when I convinced him to hire somebody, it totally freed him up. Once the couple grasped this concept, they were able to do more than one day a week with their grandkids.

When I started taking Fridays off at my own company, I felt guilty at first. I worried about people getting jealous and the message it would send. That was the wrong way to think about it, though. If you really take a day off and literally don't think about work, it will free up your spirit. It will make you easier to deal with and less likely to snap at people. I forgot about the people who were jealous because the change was so freeing, and so much peace came out of it. That's what I want for my clients to experience. Let's make that kind of change happen.

Like I've said, and I will probably repeat again, you must invest in your family. You may not think you deserve them, or like you've hurt them, or damaged your relationships, but they deserve you. They deserve the best you. That's what I'm trying to give business owners (and their loved ones) with the One-Life Game Plan™.

> You must invest in your family... they deserve the best you.

Let's say you're preparing for an important client meeting. You have likely scheduled in some prep time prior to the meeting and some time to debrief afterward. Most successful business owners make sure there is plenty of time to cover the topic thoroughly and answer any questions the client may have. Now, do you treat your family the same way? Or do you fit them in when you can, as though they are an afterthought? You should be treating your key people better than your key clients. Period. During One-Life coaching sessions, I use a proprietary planning tool that helps them get to this point.

Dr. Stephen Covey says, "effective leadership is putting first things first." As an owner, you have so many different roles. The first step with the planning tool I use is to have clients list all of their roles. Next, they rank them in order of importance. As you can imagine, the vast majority of people list their spouse and parents (or another family member) as numbers one and two. We take this list and put it next to their schedule. Do they line up? When they don't match, clients have begun to identify which of their roles can be "outsourced." I even ask them which parts of their lives have even a remote possibility of being managed by someone else. Being a parent, spouse, or sibling is a unique ability and is never mentioned as roles to be outsourced.

I will never understand how successful business owners brag to each other about how slammed they are at work and wear it around like a badge of honor. Busy is a horrible four-letter word. Have you ever counted how many men are constantly distracted by their phones out on the golf course? They're supposed to be out on the links relaxing, but they're either talking about how much they work or are glued to a screen actually working. Owners are always trying to out-busy each other because they think it's an indicator of how much their business is growing and how well it's doing. They think it's a positive thing, but it's not. In golf, you drive for show and putt for dough. Getting the longest drive is entertaining, and it is important, but the game is won on the putting green. After all, you hit more putts than drives on every hole. In business, top-line growth is for show, but what about the profits for dough? You can't always solve a problem with more sales. In fact, it may put you out of business in the long run when you stop being profitable. Instead, I encourage my clients to solve the problems and make things profitable right now, instead of striving for more sales.

Vacations, holidays, and free days

Interviews in business magazines and websites often feature owners and executives who wake up at 4 a.m. and go to bed after midnight, filling every waking moment with email after meeting after paperwork. But really, what does being busy do for you? We've already established that you're not being more productive. It's definitely not healthy for your relationships. Being busy for the sake of being busy does nothing for you. It does nothing for your business. Your "busy-ness" does not help your business.

Being busy has no inherent qualities that are going to help you personally or your business. You might be busy with activities that help your business, but nine times out of ten, those activities are not as helpful as you think they will be.

How could this possibly be? Great question. Think about how you handle emails, which we discussed in chapter one. Put a system in place so someone else can pull half your emails off the top and handle them with guidance so that everything doesn't fall on you as the owner.

Here's another example. A business owner usually starts as the lead salesman, but then years pass, and they are still shouldering that load. I've heard people say they have not developed much of a sales team because they were waiting for just the right person to come along who they were going to mentor and groom as their next lead. I'll tell you right now, that silver bullet salesperson or protégé does not exist. Put your system on paper and build a team around it. Another trap I see owners fall into is trying to rush to hire someone without a system in place. If you hire a full-time employee and pay them a ton of money, they will fail without a proper system, and you'll be even more bogged down. But if you take the time to develop a strong system and then build a group of people around it, you'll free yourself up significantly. We will go in-depth about hiring a sales manager and team in chapter five.

Harvard Business Review published an article in 2015 with the headline "Why Some Men Pretend to Work 80-Hour Weeks." In the article, Erin Reid discussed how in many professions, the expectation is for ideal employees to be "fully devoted to, and available for, the job, with no personal responsibilities or interests that interfere with this commitment to work." It goes on to say that while many men are happy to comply, work long hours, and live on the road, research suggests that a majority of men who work like this are dissatisfied. In reality, men complained about kids crying when they miss shows and games, poor health, addictions caused by their work-life, and a "general sense of feeling 'overworked and 'underfamilied.'"

Breaking away from this is not easy. It is not the norm, and you'll face resistance. In fact, it's radical—and I want my clients to be radically different. Truly successful, happy business owners are not the norm. The typical owner is stressed to the max, lives a hectic life, and doesn't even know where he or she wants to be financially because no amount of money will ever make them happy. What good is maintaining this lifestyle, which has become status-quo for some owners, when it means you're stuck with a business that drains you? What was the point of starting that business? Realizing this radical viewpoint is giving yourself permission to go rogue.

> Truly successful, happy business owners are not the norm.

Combatting the hamster-wheel mindset represents a dramatic stance in today's society. Social norms encourage owners to pump all their time, energy, and resources into the business at the expense of nearly everything else. This is exactly what fuels time creep. Going countercultural is critical. However, without deviating from the norm, you can't expect results. If you're looking to get more out of business and life, change is necessary.

During coaching sessions with clients, I make sure that we assess their "hamster wheel" situation at least once a month, so they are held accountable. It's one thing to think, "Hey, this is a great idea." It's more successful if you write your goals down and keep them in front of you. Make sure your expectations are realistic. You won't flip everything in one week. Instead, bite off a couple of things at a time. Change takes time.

Focus on the biggest payoff activities. Ask yourself, "What will free up as much time as possible?" Think creatively about who or what can help you. Your assistant or a trusted employee can probably help, and they can be even more effective with technology to assist them. There are a lot of computer programs and apps that can help out in big, time-saving ways. I've seen an app that can make handwritten cards for you. If you can use technology to write thank you cards to clients, that is a big payoff because it eliminates many hours and lets your clients know you care. However you move forward with your goals in this area, make sure they're visible so you can make sure you're making progress and coworkers can hold you accountable. Over time, you'll discover what can be thrown overboard, and you'll get so much better at saying "no."

In the business world, it's all a "go-go-go" culture. The economy has sped up, there's truth to that, but that doesn't mean we have to be out of control. Don't grind your operations to a halt, but get them under control. Think of your business as a car. A fast car that's out of control can

WHAT WOULD FREE UP AS MUCH TIME AS POSSIBLE?

cause a lot of damage, but when a car is under control, it can do a lot of wonderful things.

Maybe you've tried to change before. You might have allowed yourself a day or two off when Gerber released *E-Myth*. I know from personal experience, and from many examples I've witnessed, that it probably went really well, but before you knew it, you were right back where you started. Maybe you took a fabulous vacation with your spouse, and you realized you couldn't return to the way you had been. You came home, committed to spending more time with your spouse on a daily basis, and the first few days went great. You were on a post-vacation high! Major progress was being made, but then reality hit.

Suddenly, you had to put your amazing changes on hold to handle an unexpected situation with a major client at just the wrong time. You are disappointed with yourself, but you're looking forward to getting back into the swing of things. Except, the "swing of things" isn't the new routine you've established. The swing of things is the habit you've gotten into over the past several years: prioritizing work over everything else and giving your family the leftovers. When unexpected situations arise, stay focused on your goals. It takes a long time to establish a new set of habits.

Let's circle back to free days. When you first implement free days into your schedule, you may find yourself at a loss for how to spend them. That's because most business owners have not had a truly free day in years, and their lives and priorities now are vastly different from what they were "back in the day." Your last free day may have been spent on spring break during college (a very long time ago for myself and some readers). Chances are, the way you used to spend spring break isn't appealing to who you are now.

Approach free days with the same focused mindset you apply to buffer and focus days. The goal is to create and maintain relationships. Booking quality time and quantity time for your key relationships should be a priority for free days. This is not to say that every waking moment of your free day should be spent with family, but it should be a high priority, as it is an integral part of the free day concept.

Spending more time with your kids doesn't always leave you feeling good about yourself or where you are in your relationship with them. Family vacations can be stressful events—more *National Lampoon's Christmas Vacation* than *It's a Wonderful Life*. Similarly, not every conversation with your spouse is life-affirming. Relationships are work. They require an investment of your time and energy, just like your business. Just like any task on your to-do list at work, if you don't make time for it, improved relationships won't happen. Ignore sunk costs. Results-orientation does not serve you well in this arena.

Family businesses

We've spent a lot of time discussing family relationships in your personal life. Now, it's worthwhile to spend time talking about some of the unique challenges you encounter in a family business. Many of my clients run family businesses, but even if you don't, never intend to, and think nepotism is a bad word, this chapter will be of interest to you because chances are you'll encounter some family-run businesses within your professional network. Family dynamics tend to affect organizational structure, company culture, and how the company is viewed. They come in many types and sizes of businesses, but as different as they are, most family businesses' problems are not unique. The same challenges of mixing business and personal relationships are common to the vast majority of family businesses.

Whether family members are owners, employees, or even contractors, there are six common, yet major, tendencies that cause conflict.

1. **Unfair treatment:** First, there is the way family members treat each other. A lot of times, employees who are related treat each other worse than coworkers they are not related to. If your dad (or any relation, really) is your boss, he may be harder on you than the rest of your team. Another sticky situation is when family members belittle each other at work. This can be just as damaging to a working relationship when it is done in private as it is in front of everyone.

2. **Lack of systems:** A lot of the time, family businesses don't have enough systems in place, or they aren't as developed as non-family businesses. This can stem from either having too few things down on paper in general for the entire business or from exempting family members from these systems.

3. **Lack of communication:** This is a struggle for a lot of leaders. Those issues get magnified when it's a family business. Fearing that they will stir up family conflict, or because they assume it's not necessary, many owners do not communicate enough with employees. This can cause a lot of issues within the family in addition to the host of problems that arise when owners don't communicate enough with non-family employees.

4. **Lack of job descriptions:** The next problem isn't limited to family businesses, either: no written job descriptions. The problems can erupt on a larger scale when family dynamics are involved. This can cause responsibilities to balloon to unreasonable levels, or it can result in family members consistently underperforming and draining the team.

5. **Unrealistic expectations:** Family members have high expectations for each other, sometimes too high. When you hire someone you're related to, it's tempting to assign tasks based on the potential you think you see in them, which can cloud your judgment. There's a relationship between authority and responsibility. In less-effective family businesses, family members give each other too much authority and too little responsibility. Less commonly, family members can receive a great deal of responsibility but little authority. This tends to happen when younger children are working. There are two primary areas why expectations can soar—first, competence. Parents often expect their kids to be able to handle complex tasks with excellence.

6. **Commitment issues:** Commitment to the family trade is the other problem with the expectations parents have for their kids. When parents expect (or more accurately, assume) that children will be equally as committed to the business as they are. This is naive at best. If a family member is particularly good at his or her job, they will have a variety of other opportunities to use their talents. If the family business is not their first choice, they might disengage and cause further family frustration.

For those of you who count yourselves lucky (though others would say unfortunate) to have never worked with family, it's easy to say, "if I ever worked with my family, the first thing I'd do is set some boundaries and establish structure." Family issues are inevitably going to be brought into a family business at some point. There's no way around it. If I am in business with my brother and he's 50, then no matter what we do together in business, there is going to be 50 years of baggage there, as well. Everything in our lives, from how our parents treated us to how we treated each other as kids, is going to be right below the surface. The first step is to recognize that and take the time to work through those things.

Working with your children

I did some coaching with a father and son ownership team a while back. The son came into the business as a sales manager. He spent a lot of time on the road and routinely used the company credit card for things like gas, oil changes, and general vehicle maintenance. Those costs were acceptable and expected as part of the job. Later, he used the same card to charge new tires for his car, though. When his father found out, that purchase caused a huge rift. I didn't work with these owners until 15 years after this happened, but it still festered under the surface and occasionally above the surface when tensions were high. The father thought his son should have come to him and asked for permission to buy the tires first. The father had started the business years earlier and developed it into a multi-million dollar company, yet a huge fight exploded over $1,500 tires.

The issue was trust. The son didn't think it was a big deal. He wasn't embezzling. He'd driven thousands of miles on the company's behalf and considered it general maintenance that he needed to keep working on the road. If he had asked, his dad would have said "OK." In hindsight, it was a problem rooted in communication, but a lifetime of father-son baggage was what caused it to blow up and cause a wound that wouldn't heal.

If this happened in a non-family run business, a supervisor would have simply said, "sorry, but we don't reimburse for tires." The employee would end up covering the cost, and nobody else would have had to get involved. However, relatives bring so much emotion to a business they run together.

One of the best things you can do to avoid these situations is go over the top with communication. Everybody needs to recognize when something is a sticky issue for someone else. Within a family business, there is no such thing as "it's just business" because it gets personal real quick. I coach clients to address things when they come up immediately. Don't let issues fester because if something little comes back around months from now, things can blow up.

Another example of how working with family members can magnify a situation was when one of my clients, who ran an insurance agency, brought on his daughter to handle some marketing projects. She had been at a point in her life where she didn't know exactly what kind of career she wanted, and her father wanted to engage her in the business. She ended up being great at the job, and he enjoyed having her around. Three or four months later, though, she finished the job she was hired for and announced she was leaving. Her dad was hurt, and not just because he would miss her. He felt that he invested so much in her and was upset that she would take that knowledge and work somewhere else.

That client decided not to tell his daughter how he felt at the time. He confided later, though, that he wished he communicated with her better because the hurt stuck with him. Every time she made a career move after that, he would judge her harshly and think about how much better off she would be working in the family business. They only worked together for a few months, and it got messy enough that it clouded their relationship for quite a long time. It's a hard reality to face when owners realize they took it for granted

com•mu•ni•ca•tion

Go over the top with

COMMUNICATION.

all these years that one, or more, of their children would come aboard and take the reins when they felt ready to retire.

Even owners who have a great track record of hiring employees who aren't related to them tend to put working with their children on a pedestal. After years of watching their children overcome challenges and excel in areas of interest, parents create delusions of grandeur in regards to their adult children. They fail to think critically about how their child will operate in the specific role for which they were hired.

That's assuming they were hired for a specific role, though. This is one of the many pitfalls to avoid when your kid does join the family business. Many parents who own businesses bring children on and neglect to define their role in the company. Working a defined job provides a benchmark to measure success. Additionally, defined responsibility sets any employee up for success, and a close relative is no exception.

Incorporating your son or daughter into your company culture

Another issue to consider is how you would incorporate your son or daughter into the company culture. Many family-owned businesses have two competing cultures: the family culture and the corporate culture of non-family employees. There are two important things to consider when you hire one of your children. First, don't shortchange them on training. Just because they've been around passively "observing" for years does not mean they can skip the onboarding process. No matter how qualified any new hire is, you can never skip onboarding. The second thing you must do is prepare your other employees for the transition. Bringing in one of your children is not something to spring on existing employees. Everyone deserves to be briefed on the position your son or daughter is filling and how they fit into the team and organization as a whole. Provide your employees with the reason why you hired your son or daughter. Outline the problem that you need help with and why they are a good fit. Explain their qualifications and write down their job description for everyone to see. Last but not least, have conversations with people who will be working closely with them.

The transition won't be clean, so don't kid yourself. Recognize if things aren't working out and re-evaluate as necessary. Think about this baseball analogy, for example. If you're the manager and a roster spot opens up, how would you prepare the rest of your players if you brought in your son to play? You can say and do all the right things, but if you put him in to bat cleanup and he strikes out 50 times, he probably shouldn't be there.

Working with your spouse

Working with my spouse is an area where I have experience. The fact that I am blessed to have such an amazing wife made the transition a lot easier than it could have been. Before she started, we had a conversation about how she would have to work harder than anyone else. She showed everyone from the get-go that she was willing to take care of less-than-glamorous tasks. She also showed my employees how much she cared about them and that she wanted to make their lives easier. This process took time. We knew it wouldn't happen in a day, and it probably took about a year or so for her to earn the trust of the majority.

There will always be people who don't agree with hiring a family member. You'll overhear rumors and pick up on attitudes of dissent from time to time. These may cause you extra anxiety at home and work because you'll be overly sensitive to them at first. Odds are, though, that if you have 40 employees, two will disagree with you about anything, right? Hiring a spouse will be no different.

By definition, your spouse will have a leg up. If you bring two people in with the same degree and the same experience, if one is a stranger, and you're married to the other, who is going to have the advantage? The answer is clear. My advice, though, is to prepare your spouse for an uphill battle and be overly cautious about how you interact with them at work. I know I'm stating the obvious here, but don't show them favoritism in public. Treat them like everyone else. On second thought, go out of your way to show favor to other employees. It's imperfect at best, and there's not just one way to handle it. The key is recognizing that there will be problems and get out ahead of them. Great things could come out of it, too.

If you decide to move forward with hiring your spouse, start by establishing boundaries. Most business owners already experience boundary issues between their work and personal lives. However, owners aren't alone here. What you may not have considered is that your spouse has been experiencing the consequences that go along with time creep for years. When you work with your spouse, these problems grow exponentially.

There are two types of boundary-crossing that occur when spouses work together:

1. **Work in personal life:** This is the more common type. Letting business seep into a marriage often commonly causes a "come to Jesus moment" for spouses who work together. Whether you are business partners or your spouse is an employee, it's easy to slip into shop talk during date night. Remember, the business will take over your entire life if you let it.

2. **Personal life at work:** When marital spats leak into the workplace, watch out. Everyone feels uncomfortable. Husbands and wives argue. Even the healthiest marriages have fights. It's going to happen to you, too. There will be clipped tones, icy shoulders, and all the other consequences that come in the wake of an argument. These things will not go unnoticed by your staff.

The solution to these problems isn't perfect, quick, or easy. However, if I haven't scared you away from working with your spouse yet, my advice is to seek a marriage counselor. Don't wait; take action now even if you don't foresee issues.

Problems will arise that require an unbiased third party to resolve. You'll need help with relationship and business issues. These will take self-control and a clear action plan to make progress. If you're working with your spouse, how will you resolve to hold off on personal arguments until you get home? How do you keep your cool when you're at the office stewing over something your spouse did to upset you the night before?

My wife and I experienced some of these problems early on after I started my business. This was before she actually came on as an official employee. She had another full-time job, but I asked her to work on the books for me at night. For a variety of reasons, this was not ideal. However, the main issue was that I did not treat her as well as I should have. I fell into the trap of treating her worse than I would have treated an employee, when I should have shown extra care and concern. Now, I don't recommend bringing your spouse into the business after hours to do work that is not glamorous. You'll both become cranky, overworked, and ready to call it quits. There is no perfect scenario when working with a spouse, but that is definitely something to avoid.

Years later, when my wife started working at the office full time, we still had to do some problem-solving. She had stayed home raising our children for years. Now that she was at the office, responsibilities at home needed to be restructured. When she was a stay-at-home mom, household chores skewed toward her. Now, that division of labor no longer worked or made sense. We made adjustments over the years, and I don't think either of us regret the changes that had to be made.

Working with your siblings

Generally speaking, working with your brothers and sisters is easier to deal with than your children or spouse. Conflicts tend to be shallower, and it's easier to remain unbiased. Chances are if you didn't get along, you wouldn't find yourself in business with each other, anyway.

Family dynamics are not as entrenched with adult siblings because you (most likely) don't live under the same roof anymore. A lot of brothers and sisters get along much better later in life than they did growing up because there is a healthy distance. Depending on how close you are to your extended family, you might see your sibling and his or her family outside the office weekly, biweekly, or monthly.

There is still potential for negative effects at work, though. Employees may detect unwitting preferential treatment. This is usually not as obvious to the owner as with a child or spouse because they aren't thinking about it as much. It's easier to forget about and not account for nepotism. However, it will always be perceived by employees outside the family.

Sometimes nepotism is not bad

Let's just put that out there. Nepotism is not always a bad word. More is caught than taught. Children who have grown up in the business, been around the office, heard about it at dinner, even worked there during high school will know how to do a business. My children, for example, know it all comes down to taking care of customers because my wife and I are constantly having those discussions at home.

I cannot stress enough that you need to address stigmas associated with nepotism with any family member before bringing them aboard. Set some goals with them, and make sure they understand how high expectations will be for them.

If one of your children wants to work for you, it's best to be honest. Admit that it may be easier for them to start their career somewhere else in the short term. If they choose to work for you, everybody is going to watch every move they make. In the long run, it makes sense to bring them on if you think they could eventually be an owner. Maybe you'd even sell them your business for a cheaper price, someday. Membership has its privileges.

Team Management and Corporate Culture

My clients tend to have successful businesses before they start the One-Life Game Plan™. I'm never surprised by what they have: millions in profits, large staffs, multiple properties, busy schedules, etc. I am always surprised, though, by what they don't have: an organizational chart. Since my role is to help them problem solve, grow, and run more efficiently, the first thing I often ask for is a chart ranked in order of authority that demonstrates their company's chain of command. Yet, I get so many soft answers in response to this request.

Some clients say they made one years ago, but it doesn't reflect their current situation. Or, they'll say they have a clear structure set up, it's just not written down. They're usually not prepared, though, when I put a blank sheet of paper in front of them and ask for it again. When they force themselves to get it down on paper, it gives everything more clarity. They risk organizational confusion by not having a chart, and the bottom line is that they're wasting time and money.

The first chart I want clients to make should reflect what is going on in real-time in their company. Sometimes it may be a good exercise to make a separate chart with your leadership team that includes your ideal structure. However, documenting what things are like in your company here and now forces you to think about your organization and make decisions.

In a smaller business, it's not uncommon to find individuals with titles that don't represent the scope of their work. There are two sides to this coin. The first is the possibility of duplicate work. If you struggle with project overruns, or you're consistently running behind schedule despite having the correct employees on a project, you might have individuals doing the same work. On the other side of the coin, it is possible that tasks are falling through the cracks. Either way, projects are not getting done efficiently.

It's pretty common for business owners to start this process and realize they're operating with outdated reporting roles. When you start a business, everyone reports to the owner. That's not practical anymore when you grow to 30 employees. It's not healthy to have too many people under you or any one person. When you map it out, it becomes obvious who has too many reportees and where the problems exist.

The owner is not divorcing from his or her people by making employees report to someone else. Sometimes owners still have to go down to talk to the guy on the loading dock, but that employee can't seek the owner out over every issue. After you have an organizational chart, it will become clear that you need clear job descriptions. If you don't have them, or they are too generic, that won't work. Any business bigger than a handful of employees needs them. Anytime you want to scale, you need clarity. Organizational charts and job descriptions are tools you need to help you see weaknesses, such as where people have too broad or too narrow positions.

When you encounter a position that has a narrow scope, it can be helpful to include that person in the decisions being made. Give that person the new job description and ask them what else they are currently doing. The point is not to assign fault here, but often they are the best people to help you get the most suitable job description for their position down on paper with guidance. Another way to handle this situation is to identify someone in your company who is good at writing and documenting. Have them facilitate the process by shadowing your staff and documenting what they do to help you come up with a description.

This process takes time, which is why most business owners need to be sold on this idea. Sometimes owners don't value organizational charts because they associate them with huge corporations, which they often started their own businesses to escape. After my clients start seeing the value in organizational charts, they realize that they are just the beginning. In the end, they'll be building a system to grow on and move forward as a company.

MVV: Mission, vision, and values

These three items provide the answer to all of your "why" questions. Why do you do what you do? Why do your employees do what they do? Why should you implement the changes we've discussed throughout the book? Why do your clients choose to work with you? Why do you choose to work with your clients?

Owners, leaders, employees, and customers pay a lot of lip service to mission, vision, and values. So much, in fact, that it is easy for the meaning to get lost. Before we go further, let's pause to get on the same page with what these terms mean:

Mission Statement

This is how you plan to represent your vision to the world through your operations. What do you do for your clients? This should explain how your products and services impact your clients' lives.

Vision

This is the large-scale vision for your business. You may want to impact the world. How do you want to affect everyone who comes into contact with your organization (from clients to advisors to your mailman)? This is who your organization wants to be on the very broadest level.

Values

These are your Ethics. Here you have the keywords that make up your values: kindness, quality, respect, innovation, etc.

I would estimate that 75 percent of my coaching clients don't come in with mission, vision, or value statements. They may have some semblance, but usually, they don't make sense. We don't need flowery language here. These should be the guts of your company. What are you in business to do?

For example, a friend of mine owns a healthcare company whose mission is to "be a blessing." Everything falls under that. It sticks out to me because it's short and easy to remember. Another advantage is that it's easy to measure. Everyone in the company asks themselves if what they're doing is a blessing or not.

Remove the clutter, and don't just write the words that you think need to be included. You don't want any words in your mission statement that you aren't actually doing. Eliminate the buzz words, too. You want this to be timeless. Let's be honest with ourselves. Most businesses are not going to change the world. You're just not going to do that. So what can you do? Cut the crap; make this short and memorable. Otherwise, it will get buried and won't work. In his book *The Advantage: Why Organizational Health Trumps Everything Else in Business*, Patrick Lencioni says a lot of businesses fall into the trap of writing convoluted statements that aren't effective. He compares them to legalese and calls them "corporate-ese." They're pointless if nobody knows what they're saying. Less is more.

Mission, vision, and values must be repeated. Constantly. If you feel like you're beating a dead horse, then you're doing it right. Have some fun with them, be creative, and plan some surprise contests. At a staff meeting, hand out cash to people who can say your mission or values. See who knows them out

> Mission, vision, and values must be repeated. Constantly.

of the blue. The more it is repeated, the more ingrained it becomes. Simply repeating it is insufficient. Living it is key. When you are pointing out wins and successes around the office, wrap them into how they relate to your overall MVV. Explain how your losses hurt your MVV. While many companies have these things, most fall short in applying these principles. We like to focus on making things practical. Having a great mission statement on your website can help prospective customers understand your business. They can also attract talented employees. Ultimately, though, your MVV will have the biggest impact on your staff. A blurb on your website is far less valuable than an MVV that permeates your company culture at every level, from assistant to CEO.

I have refined my own company's MVV over the years, and each new draft is a long process. When clients sit down across from me without anything, we start by taking out a blank sheet of paper. I ask them to brainstorm words that they think describe their business to people. My goal is to keep them talking as long as possible while I keep writing. Once we get up to about 30 words, we start paring them down. When we have ten words left, we talk them through before finally refining those down to five. I believe three to five words gives you a solid jumping-off point.

Here are some of the words and phrases we came up with at the Plack Group:

- Innovative

- Better

- All about you

- Most trusted advisor

- Team

- Wisdom

- Simplicity

This was our starting point when my leadership team and I asked ourselves those "why" questions. We used those to come up with our vision statement: to better the lives of our clients, our team members, and their families in a way that honors our Creator.

Business owners are usually too close to their operations to write their own MVV effectively. Bringing in a facilitator during this process is a wise decision. If you can't have an outside person help, pick someone else within the company to facilitate. This could be an opportunity to encourage and coach someone in this area.

While you're creating your company's MVV, consider its value to new employees. Create a page called "How we do things here" for anyone who is new to read. Some businesses have these on their walls. Think of them as your office's Ten Commandments. Don't get bogged down with having ten, though. We have nineteen. Getting these down on paper helps the community-building process.

It pains me when I walk into a business, and I can tell that its employees don't know the "why" behind what they do there. I'm not suggesting they don't know what the company sells or that the employees are bad at what they've been tasked to do. My point is that when you walk into a bagel shop, do the people behind the counter know what a good day is supposed to look like in their position? Do they know what sets the company they work for apart? Writing these things down helps get them up to speed.

> Does your team know what sets the company they work for apart?

People hesitate in this area because they have seen so many poor examples of company values. Most people don't read books on this topic like I do. Writing your MVV is a hard concept. That's why it's my job to help them get started, so they can end up where they want to be.

The Plack Group's MVV is not perfect, and I'm not perfect in implementing and living our values every day. In fact, I had an employee call me out years ago on an action I took that did not fall under our MVV. She thought I might get upset at her for bringing it up, but I actually had the opposite reaction. She was right about what she said, and I appreciate the fact that she brought it to my attention.

The goal of your company's MVV should be to set up consistency. A solid MVV gets all your employees on the same side. Imagine you have a group of people trying to pull something heavy, such as a fridge, with ropes. If they were all on different sides pulling in different directions, they wouldn't go anywhere. If they are all on the same side, though, they make progress. As an owner, you have to ask yourself at the end of the day if you've moved things in the right direction, at least a little bit.

Your employees need to know what you expect from them. They need to know what game they are playing. If I show up to play basketball and the rest of my team is playing softball, I'm not going to be ready. Having an MVV, and communicating it effectively, gets commitment from the people who are working in the trenches for you on a daily basis. There is a tendency for entrepreneurs not to have an MVV because that's why big businesses do, but to grow a business, you have to get procedures in place and be consistent.

Consistency is what makes some of the major fast-food chains successful. I could start working at Chick-fil-A today and know how to make a chicken sandwich by the end of my first shift, and it would taste and look the same as at your local restaurant. This has nothing to do with how good of a cook I am, but rather because they have a system down on paper. They have pictures on the wall of where everything goes and what order to put things on the sandwich. You can't expect every employee to think like an owner or know how the owner wants everything, but you can communicate

To grow
a business,
you have to
**get procedures
in place**
and be
consistent.

your expectations. What I love about MVV is that they are above everything. They are about more than how to assemble a sandwich; they're over that. Your MVV tells employees what they are signing up for when they work for you. If they don't like the mission, then they don't have to work for you.

Communicating your MVV

There are many poor examples of mission statements out there that give this game-changing element a bad name. Even worse is the misconception that once they're written, companies just need to slap them on the walls, and they're done. You may have a beautifully crafted MVV, but it won't be effective if it's not communicated. The first step is getting it in front of people.

The next step is that you have to talk about it. It tells your employees where the company is today and where it is going. It should also motivate them to want to be on board. The leader's job is to tell employees what their role will be in getting there.

Let's load up the family van and take a pretend road trip to Disney World. When you start driving, the kids are ecstatic. They've got the snacks, the screens, the stories— everything they need to last hours on end in the van. Not long after you set the cruise control, though, somebody asks the dreaded question: "Are we there yet?" You can laugh it off the first couple of times, but the question starts coming more frequently and in a whinier tone. You don't have to have much imagination to guess what this is doing to morale in the van. The family is getting cranky. You have a few options. You could punch the cruise button a few more times in hopes of getting there faster. You could match the mood and become short-tempered. Or, you could be a proactive family leader. Remind the kids who is at the finish line: Mickey Mouse!

That's what a true leader does on a family vacation or in the office. Keep your people motivated about the destination. Tell your employees, "here is where we're going, we have a place for you, and we care." Even the best MVV can fall apart if leaders can't get commitment from staff. Don't waste your time writing the MVV if you're not going to preach it. Lack of communication in this process creates a vacuum. Your people will come up with a mission statement of their own.

> Keep your people motivated about the destination.

Sometimes it will be a good one, but more often, it will be a detriment to the company. Employees who only think about themselves will pull in one direction, those who are loyal to you will pull in the other, and those who just come to collect a paycheck will be left to decide which side to join. Everyone will be pulling in different directions, and your company will experience organizational confusion.

One-Life coaching sessions spend a lot of time on this. We are innovative in this effort, and I've had clients referred based on needing to work on an MVV alone. Some ask to see the Plack Group's MVV first, but I usually wait. Ours works for us, but every business owner needs to find the one that works for their goals and their team. Ours isn't the best, but it works for us. Since we actually have something, I'd guess it at least puts us in the top 15 percent of companies. I encourage clients to explore what other companies put out there. Leading organizations have clarity and should be the North Star for companies who need direction.

Before you're ready to roll an MVV out to your staff, have a 12-month communication plan in place. Hammer on it, put it in peoples' hands, put it up on the walls, and revisit it at meetings. Set up your leadership team to be its evangelists, and remember the work will never be done. Leaders must constantly motivate people to get where they want them to go and how they want them to get there. Remember not to overwhelm your people with information, though. An MVV should be short and to the point. You can only put so many things in a users' manual and answer so many questions in an FAQ section. You can't possibly get to everything at once, but if you know the values and take them on yourself, there is a higher likelihood your employees will know how to respond.

The reason you have to motivate your employees so much has its roots in human nature. According to Gallup, in 2018, the percentage of "engaged" workers in the United States was at one of its highest recorded levels. The percentage of employees "involved in, enthusiastic about, and committed to their work and workplace" came in at 34 percent. That's fantastic, right? What this means is that slightly more than one-third of your employees will be intrinsically motivated by your MVV in the long run. Don't forget about the "actively disengaged," though. Workers who have "miserable work experiences" were as high as 13 percent nationally. Some of the employees in this category may be on your payroll and could be hurting your company. Not everybody has the interest of the owner, and to think that they do is completely wrong. Some people just have jobs and don't have to care much about the success of the company. Your employees don't have to be willing to give blood for your company, but given the right MVV, you can have people do a great job for you during the day and go home feeling like they did a great job. Set up a situation where everyone can succeed.

A larger focus on team member engagement is what often comes out of the MVV process. The biggest thing that comes out of these coaching sessions with owners is leaders who realize the importance of people. Their employees aren't just tools to get things done. They are the future because every owner is in the "people business." Developing people is the key to scaling a business. Owners have to help their people move forward. We have got to serve them, coach them, and give them strength-finder assessments to understand them and each other. Everybody is diverse. Our job as owners is to figure out how we can get them to succeed in their role with your company. That's how to grow a culture of people who will serve your customers.

I'd bet money that if you go through this process, you will see employees improve. After a few months, my clients typically report that their staffs operate better as a team. One of the biggest challenges related to an MVV that I helped a company overcome was a government contractor that had about 100 employees nationwide. The problem was that every employee was operating solo, isolated in government outposts across the country. It's a challenge to have a strong company culture when you don't see people on a regular basis. After the company's owner and leadership team went through the MVV process, employees realized that they were a part of a team and something bigger than themselves. When you go through this, you invite your employees to move in the direction your company is going. That is the power of people. Most want to do good at the end of the day. The power of the organization is leading its people so they are prepared and pulling in the same direction.

Coaching employees

An initial step involved in getting your people on your organization's side is coaching them to move forward in their desired career paths. One of the first things you'll have to do is help your employees identify their own strengths and weaknesses. This task sounds like a lot of fluff, but most people lack the self-awareness to accurately assess themselves. I help my clients to tap into their strengths and coach them on their weaknesses. I never ask them what they are, though, because they won't know. Either people aren't equipped to answer that, or they provide a canned response.

Instead, I prefer to use a personality profiling system. There are a lot of good assessments out there. Here are a few I recommend:

- StrengthsFinder

- DiSC

- Kolbe

- Myers-Briggs

- Enneagram

These profiles can be incredibly effective tools to help employees self-identify their major personality traits. Most of these cost less than $50. The best profiling systems include clear information to help people apply newly-attained knowledge and apply it to their work. Sometimes I use multiple assessments because they are all a little different, and I want as much information as I can about people. I don't just use them with my coaching clients, either. I use them to get to know the people I work with because they make the difference. The worst mistake an employer can make is to hire someone and have to fire them six months later after investing all that time and money in recruiting, training, and paying their salary.

When the assessment is done, and the data is in, the most important part is going over results with people. I suggest having the person summarize their report to their team. Ask a new hire to go over their strengths during a staff meeting one week and the rest of the staff to talk about theirs the following week. One of my favorite systems is the Enneagram because it breaks down if someone falls below, at, or above average with nine personality types. It then describes the positive and negative traits of that personality and gives advice on how that person might perform at work. For example, if you're a perfectionist, then at your best, you can work with others on a team, but at your worst, you tend to shun other people. If you want to learn more about it, I suggest reading *The Road Back to You: An Enneagram Journey to Self-Discovery* by Ian Morgan Cron and Suzanne Stabile.

Personality profiling systems can also be useful for creating and maintaining teams. This can help reduce conflict between employees. Digital agencies should pay close attention to this: in an industry relying so heavily on the collaborative effort of teams, it is extremely important to have a sense of the strengths and weaknesses of individual team members to enhance communication and strengthen the team.

Leaders who are successful, and coach their employees need to understand their teams, how they work together, and what individuals do well. A lot of times, employees are placed on a team without being given a choice in the matter or a chance to transfer. That's why sitting down and going over the results from these profiling systems is so powerful. Working on a team is universal. Sometimes, not even the owner has the luxury of changing or creating teams because they have to make do with the people they have. So get vulnerable with each other. The conversation about these results is the transformative piece. You're likely going to have one person on each team who doesn't like sharing in this kind of way, but the leader's job is to justify the process.

More businesses would do this regularly, but nobody is making them, and many bosses don't see the urgency. Those who have these conversations with their teams see the value immediately, though. If an employee is having a good day, then they are going to feel better and be a whole lot more effective. If they get chewed out by their boss, they are going to be worthless for the rest of the day. A lot of bosses take that tact, and the negative impact is tangible. So trust me on investing in your people this way, and you'll see a much harder working team.

I've had clients ask me if personality profiling systems and the discussions around them can be something they farm out to division heads. I don't believe that would be effective, as owners need to be the champions of this process. I tell clients they really need to find religion on this idea. They've got to provide the initial energy and sell it as a worthy cause. That's why owners shouldn't direct people to take care of it and step away. The expression "leaders go first" is as true here as anywhere else. If you want people to be vulnerable, you have to go first. It won't happen without the leader's example.

In a smaller business, working closely with a team is par for the course. Hopefully you'll be able to retain many of these employees for a long period of time. One of the keys to employee retention is also a byproduct of employee retention: care. This process shows concern for them. Get acquainted with your team. When you're in a leadership position, it's a gift, but there are a lot of responsibilities that go with it. Don't get wrapped up in your position as head of the company. It's not about lording authority over people or having them serve you. It's about you serving people and seeing people in your organization do better.

There is not a special technique that you can learn in a book. You actually have to care. Another thing I love about Chick-fil-A is that you always get a smile from someone. If an employee smiles at you and shows that they care, no matter where you're shopping or eating, then they are in the top one percent. You can't have a successful business if you don't smile and show you care sometimes. Based on the clients I have worked with, I can tell you that this does not come naturally for some owners. Sometimes I have to coach them through a process from looking at their staff members as tools to looking at them as people. You probably wouldn't be this far in the book if you didn't care about your people. Not just your customers, either. They are important, but make an effort to get to know your employees, their family situations, and what they care about. Now, if you have a 500-person team, you can't do it all by yourself, but you can invest this way in your leadership team, and they can carry the message.

I like to get clients started in this process by having them write notes to employees when they see something they appreciate. In chapter one, I mentioned an app that can make handwritten notes for you. That's not what I'm talking about here. Keep some stationery and pens nearby and get yourself into the habit of writing three or four short notes a week. Even in a small company, the owner is the "big boss" to his or her employees. The words of the leader ring loud and long in the hearts of the team. A three-sentence note goes a long way. Take it a step further, though, and mail it to your employees' homes. That way, they can proudly show it to their families. It may end up on their fridge, and it will definitely last a long time because people don't throw thank you notes away. I don't care what someone's StrengthsFinder test may say, everyone needs praise. In CEO, the "E" stands for encouragement. Pay attention to people, and they will do a better job for you. Everybody needs a regular dose of something positive.

Personality profiles can help you find people's strengths, and that's a great starting point for what to provide feedback on. Ask your employees if the company is encouraging their strengths, and if they're not sure, provide them with some opportunities. A lot of people consider this "soft" and ephemeral, but what I've found is that it's the right thing to do. When you do the right thing, good things are going to come. Some people will burn you no matter what because they're absolute takers, but they're 1-in-100. You will help the overwhelming majority move forward.

Help them do better for themselves, and they will do better for the company.

The Feedback Loop

Many business owners fall short when it comes to providing employees with constructive feedback. A surprising number of owners have no regular feedback loop or system. They either have one on a schedule but fail to keep up with it, or they take care of this haphazardly. The first step is simply creating a feedback system that can be maintained. Second, it's critical to create written feedback. While this can and should be paired with face-to-face conversation, providing written feedback gives employees something to review. Here is the simple structure that should become routine.

Annual review

These should only deal with the largest-scale issues.

Monthly feedback

More detailed than the annual review, monthly feedback is often eschewed for quarterly feedback. However, monthly feedback is a more natural rhythm for many people. The problem is that by the time a quarter wraps up, most people have forgotten everything that was said in the last meeting. Meeting monthly means that the last meeting is still fairly fresh in everyone's mind, thus enabling you to see the long-term cause and effect.

Weekly wrap-in

Setting the tone for the week by meeting on a Monday is really useful. Whatever day you decide to meet, though, it is important that the group comes together once a week to keep everyone up to date on current projects and issues. On the task level, you see what is really going on in the business. Receiving updates on projects on the task level is critical.

I see so much reluctance to adopt these routines because owners don't know how they'll sustain this cycle. So I ask them: is everything just the way you want it to be with your team? Nobody ever says, "yes, it's perfect!" Well then, if you want things to change, don't you have to give your people feedback? It's ultimately a relationship issue between managers and team members, yet so many leaders dread or simply do a terrible job with feedback. If you want people on your team to hang around, you'd better start this process. I like to keep my employees out of the want ads by taking care of them, so they don't want another job.

By definition, businesses change, and leaders constantly have to improve their practices. If you have a high employee turnover, how are you going to move forward? On the other side, if you have staff members who aren't right for their positions, then you have to make those hard decisions. Have a conversation about performance. Make sure to listen to what they have to say and draw out their side of the problem. What is holding an employee back from meeting a standard? If they're doing something wrong, give them something positive. If they're not happy, they won't perform close to someone who is happy.

Now it's time to add some measurable goals, objectives, or key performance indicators (KPIs) into the feedback loop. The more involved an employee is in creating his or her own KPIs, the more likely he or she is to improve performance. For higher-level employees, this is a fairly familiar process. In these cases, the difficult part is encouraging them to push themselves in order to prevent plateaus. This could involve developing leadership skills or being trained on something new. Here is the structure I recommend having in place for KPIs.

Daily

Every single employee at the organization, from the janitorial staff to the CEO, must have daily KPIs. Without them, people come into work with no direction and no way to measure if they have done a good job. In addition, work toward everyone setting their own daily KPIs, from interns to the owner.

Weekly

The majority of employees will have weekly KPIs. If you have teams that meet weekly, encourage them to briefly review if they met their KPIs. If they didn't, have them come up with a plan to meet them for the upcoming week.

Monthly

The majority of employees will also have monthly KPIs. These can be reviewed similarly to weekly goals.

Annual

The annual review is a long-standing office tradition. Use these as an opportunity to place an employee's performance within the broader scope of the company, in the past, present, and future.

While traditional top-down reviews are useful, they fail to take into account the employee's point of view. A trend that I encourage my clients to adopt has been toward 360-degree reviews. These combine insight from the employee as well as insight from the manager. Not only is this a great idea, but it gets to the heart of reporting. I have found that seeing what employees have to say about their own performance is one of the most enlightening sources of information available to an owner. This enables you to pinpoint problems with more precision than you would have otherwise. Even if employees themselves have a hard time articulating what the problem is, their assessment of themselves provides a window into where the discrepancy lies.

For example, one of my clients had an employee who was a team player and a fantastic designer; however, he consistently failed to communicate with clients. This senior design employee performed extremely well and got along with the rest of the staff, yet this one area was a constant issue. During a 360-degree review, having the employee unpack the issue shed some light on its roots. The employee said, "our clients don't want to be bothered, and they are hard to reach." Now it was clear as day that this employee's misconceptions were influencing his performance in a critical area. The conversation got to the heart of the issue that had been plaguing the business for months, and now it was solvable.

Another important note on the topic of annual reviews is to make sure they provide an idea of the destination for the next year. The journey needs to be charted in monthly, weekly, and daily KPIs. Put the responsibility for setting up these plans on the employee being reviewed as much as possible.

I've tried my best to sell you on the importance of a feedback loop. However, if you are not sold on the relationship and employee perspective side of the review, think about it as a financial benefit. Your payroll percentage is your biggest investment. Don't you want to maximize that? You can't protect that investment if your people aren't happy. It's not your job to please them, but it is helpful to know why they're not happy. This process may also make them reconsider the job they're doing and "free them up" to do something else that makes them happy. Maybe you're still on the fence about the sensitive nature of these conversations, but if there is a problem that you could fix in your business, wouldn't you? If your car always had terrific gas mileage and all of a sudden its miles per gallon went down, you would take it to the shop to figure out the problem. You've got to do the same with your people.

You can't afford to not have these conversations with your employees. One client who implemented this type of feedback loop was amazed at how a simple conference with an employee solved a problem that immediately improved efficiency. He noticed productivity had been down for one of his data entry specialists. When he asked her what was going on and got her talking, she mentioned something was wrong with her keyboard. The owner heard this, ordered a $40 keyboard, and the problem was solved. If it was that simple, why didn't she just ask for a new keyboard when the problem started? He asked her some more questions, and it turns out that she wanted to be frugal and save the company money. Every week that she had been using the old keyboard, her productivity went down, so the owner thought it was worth the easy fix.

When I heard this story, another issue stuck out to me. Why did she think the company would want her to work that way? Why was that alright with her? I would want her to speak up and get it fixed on day one. She didn't understand the game the company was playing. The owner wasn't playing to save money. He was playing to be effective. In her defense, she thought she was doing the right thing. That tells me that the owner wasn't projecting his true values to his team.

With an effective feedback loop, every employee should feel free to approach the leader with an obstacle. This is especially true as more of the workforce works remotely and could be spread around the country. Leaders of those companies should aim to hold a 15-minute check-in meeting with their staff every morning. Every week they should meet for an hour or two to go over big-picture items. However, often you decide to meet, get into the rhythm, and stay consistent. Additionally, schedule one-on-ones with employees. Try to get in three each week. The more frequently you can get to all the individuals on your team, the better. Everyone should feel comfortable asking for help. Owners should want their employees to throw up a flag if there is a problem because it should be fixed as quickly as possible.

Change isn't easy. It's OK to ask for help from somebody like a consultant or coach. Someone from outside can provide a new, unbiased perspective. We've worked with thousands of companies and can offer a lot of new ideas. Whoever you decide to work with, it may be beneficial for it to be someone who is not from your industry. Once your company is beyond starting up, industry expertise only goes so far. If you want to rise above your competition, you need to do things differently. I have learned a lot from different industries that I bring back and apply to my business. I've taken a page out of books from the automotive industry, from FedEx, even Amazon. For example, Amazon does a terrific job of giving customers confidence in their services. If I order a package from Amazon and they tell me it will arrive on Tuesday, then I know it will arrive on Tuesday. Now, why is that? I haven't spoken with anyone from the company. Customers are so confident because Amazon excels at communication. Consumers used to gain confidence in companies by going to a mall, talking to their employees, and looking at the flashy displays. That's how people used to judge where to spend their money. Generally speaking, people have more confidence in a product they buy from a big store versus a street vendor. In the era of e-commerce, Amazon has my confidence because they do things like send multiple email updates on my order's status, take pictures when they deliver a package, and ask me to rate my experience with every item and delivery. In my business, we work on big projects that take a lot of time. I can learn from Amazon by communicating better with my customers about their project's status. That way, they know we are giving them attention even though they can't see it every day.

CHAPTER 3
Accountability

ACCOUNTABILITY IS THE KEY to turning an idea or a wish into something that actually happens. I believe it's more beneficial to spend time on personal accountability here than corporate accountability. This is especially important to owners because there aren't a lot of people out there who know what it's like to own a business.

You've got to start with being accountable to yourself. Holding yourself to a standard of integrity and character is step one. If you are not honest with yourself, who will be? Not your employees. Since you're the boss, they won't always be honest with you. Probably not your friends, either.

Unless your social circle includes other business owners, your friends—try as they might—will struggle to relate to the problems you deal with every day. They think you're living the dream and couldn't possibly have anything to complain about. After all, you own a successful company, right? That's why you have got to force yourself to take a good look at how you are conducting your business and your life. Know what your responsibilities are to your business, your family, and to yourself.

First, be honest. If you are truly honest, then you have to be humble. The facts leave no other option. We all have room to grow, and this is a foundational truth for accountability. Second, listen. Accountability involves letting others speak into your life. You have to hear from others for this to happen. Being open to their input and putting in the effort to hear what others are saying is necessary to this process. Think about who can hold you accountable in the areas we focus on in the One-Life Game Plan™.

Every business owner needs a team to succeed. This doesn't necessarily mean employees or partners, although, they can certainly be part of the team. Think about people from various spheres of life and business whom you can trust. Business owners frequently overlook the need for a team outside of work. However, having people like this on your side can provide wisdom and perspective in the many situations where knowledge is required.

❶ The Expert

Develop a relationship with someone in your field who is more experienced at whatever you're doing. Pick his or her brain whenever possible. This person should be someone you can call when you're completely stumped with a technical problem.

❷ The Big-Picture Person

For many people, this is a spouse. However, it can be any trusted person who can put things into perspective. The big-picture person can look at both your business and your personal life with clarity and perspective. Trust this person to help with decisions that relate to both areas. He or she will become your right-hand man (or woman).

❸ The Fellow Business Owner

Find someone who has a business on a similar scale in another industry. This person understands what it's like to be in the trenches. It can be helpful to swap business wisdom you've picked up or just commiserate when necessary. Other people who know the unique demands on an owner can provide a valuable network of support. You can meet these people through professional networking groups or simply from getting involved in the local business scene. It helps if there is something additional linking you together, whether it's religious beliefs, community engagement, or a hobby. It's necessary to repeat that so few people understand what it really requires to be a business owner. The relationships you have with your clients and employees are unique. Other owners are in the same boat and can be useful for accountability in your personal life, such as making time for your family and keeping yourself healthy. Choose people who are committed to the same things you are, obviously. The overwhelming majority of owners aren't in a position that is sustainable. Don't take advice from people at the end of their ropes, but from fellow owners you can respect.

❹ Someone Who Shares Your Values

This person may attend your church or otherwise share your personal values. While some (or even all, if you're lucky) of the other team members may also have similar values, choose a separate team member who is already living out those values in specific ways. This doesn't have to be a fellow business owner. In fact, it's better if this is someone who is separate from that sphere. For a biblical example, refer to the relationship between Nathan and David in 2 Samuel, chapter 12. Nathan and David shared the same religion and the same commitment to the nation of Israel. Nathan was a close advisor to David and was not hesitant to call him out when necessary. David could trust Nathan's advice because of their shared set of values.

❺ Financial Professionals

Keeping your personal finances on track (including retirement planning) requires oversight and accountability. Your advisory team can be an invaluable resource, not only in the expertise they provide, but in their continued involvement in your unique situation.

❻ Mentors and Coaches

Coaching has a great deal in common with mentoring. However, coaching has an eye on the bottom line. Paying for it keeps you invested and accountable. You'll have automatic motivation to follow through on the changes you come up with jointly. Coaching gives you the freedom to be 100 percent focused on what your business needs. If you use coaching services that are holistic, then you have even more freedom to take a comprehensive look at what you are doing.

❼ Spouse and Family

Having a partner definitely keeps you accountable. Even children are quick to point out hypocrisy. Anyone with children knows that they are a surprisingly tough crowd.

When I bring up accountability with clients, they don't always see the business value. It can also seem like a scary topic. It's difficult, if not impossible, to measure. And it's relationship-based. Test this concept, though, and you'll see being personally accountable helps you achieve your goals. Accountability differentiates leaders. The most successful leaders are accountable to the people they lead. Putting yourself out there isn't easy. It requires commitment and leaves you vulnerable.

We need accountability in our lives, so we will follow through. It's human nature to say one thing and do another. Or maybe you set a goal with the best intentions, but then you just forget about it. Let's use weight loss as an example since it is such a common desire for people. I can say I want to lose 10 pounds, but it won't happen unless I take action. If there is no plan, there is a problem. The most successful weight loss programs, such as Weight Watchers or Jenny Craig, build accountability into their process.

It takes humility and vulnerability to ask someone to hold you accountable. If I want someone to hold me accountable for losing weight, they can serve me by calling me out on how I eat and drink. They might text me and say, "was that burger the best choice at lunch?" Or "watch how much you drink this weekend, those beers add up." On my end, I would need to open up to them about when I struggle with eating. After 7 p.m., I tend to go off the rails with snacks. I need something salty, something sweet, repeat. If I invite you in like this, now your accountability is on my mind when I reach for those chips.

During One-Life coaching sessions, my clients fill out monthly goals. Sometimes they come up with 20 things ranging from improving how much their company invoices, their desire to read a book, or writing down their daily to-do lists. Out of those, clients pick what they want me to hold them accountable for. That way, they know I'm going to ask them about it and keep bringing it up.

When you know someone is going to call you out on something, you will do it. You've got to have the relationship, though. Your accountability partner should be someone you know cares about you and wants to see you do well. If that's not there, it will be like a bell clanging in an empty auditorium. Additionally, you've got to want to be held accountable. Otherwise, you'll just get annoyed.

One client asked me to hold him accountable for having a regular date night with his wife. When I brought it up at our next meeting, he gave me some excuse about a babysitter falling through. With that in mind, we decided it would be worth investing time in finding a consistent babysitter instead of calling one the night before. I also told him to make sure to put it on the schedule, or it won't happen. I didn't want him to feel like I was scolding him. Don't beat an accountability partner over the head if they struggle with the issue. Accountability is putting something in front of them that they said they wanted to do. Remind them, and then if they're not successful, suggest some ideas.

Accountability partnerships work differently depending on the people involved and what their goals are. Recently, I was having a discussion with a friend about faith and how we value having a regular quiet time with God. We both needed to be more disciplined in this area of our lives and decided to hold each other accountable. All we do is text each other every morning with a simple "Y" or "N" depending on if we had a quiet time that day. No explanation is necessary. It doesn't matter how we spend that quiet time, the important part is that it happens. Most days, we trade "Y" messages. There are occasional "N" texts, and that is when we check in to see what is going on. Usually it's not a big deal, but if either of us goes a week without that time with God, it would lead to a more serious conversation.

> Staying disciplined in your personal life is important for a business owner.

The key to accountability partnerships that work is realizing it's a two-way street. I've got to want to be held accountable, and so do they. You couldn't just walk up to someone you know, tell them that they look pudgy, and expect them to drop weight. If I don't want someone to check in with me about my health, this person would just seem like a jerk. I've got to invite them in, and they have to care enough to follow up. If they forget, they may not be a great friend. Finding someone who understands what you want is valuable.

Staying disciplined in your personal life is important for a business owner. Lack of accountability outside the office can lead to a lack of structure in the workplace. I could take all the time off work that I want because I own the company. If an employee doesn't show up, they have a manager whose job is to hold them accountable. Nobody counts my hours or gives me a set amount of personal days every year. The ability to come and go as I please can be a beautiful thing, but it can turn ugly without guardrails. I don't typically see successful owners who don't put in the hours. It usually turns ugly because nobody approves an owner's overtime and they work too long. Remember the 20-percent rule?

> Lack of accountability outside the office can lead to a lack of structure in the workplace.

Do you own your business? Or does your business own you? Every owner needs someone to ask them those questions. It's possible that the office is in order, and even that employees are happy, but that doesn't mean the big boss is happy or healthy. I've sat across from many successful owners who have not seen a doctor in years. My question is usually, "are you doing what is important or what is urgent?"

Dr. Stephen Covey adapted the Eisenhower Matrix to make a chart that illustrated this point. A lot of things on a business owner's plate are important. These are things that are necessary to deal with, such as long-term planning and relationship building, that can take up a lot of time but aren't pressing. Urgent items, such as crises or deadline-driven projects, need to be handled immediately. Owners should be prioritizing most of their time with matters that are urgent *and* important. If someone walks into my office carrying a gun, it is urgent and important that I deal with it right away. However, sometimes things seem urgent, such as answering an email or an employee complaint. If you spend too much time working on these, you don't have time to

THE EISENHOWER MATRIX

	URGENT	NOT URGENT
IMPORTANT	**Do** Do it now.	**Decide** Schedule a time to do it.
NOT IMPORTANT	**Delegate** Who can do it?	**Delete** Eliminate it.

deal with anything important. Things that aren't urgent or important should never be on an owner's to-do list because they are complete wastes of time.

If owners don't have someone to hold them accountable, the same pattern can emerge in their lives outside the office. I tell my clients they have to be humble to be held accountable, and they have to be transparent enough to ask. I worked with a seasoned business owner who expressed his desire to be home more in the evenings. During our next meeting I asked him how many nights that week he had been home by 6 p.m. He told me he worked late every night that week and made excuses for the busy season he was in. I didn't come down hard on him. Instead, I worked with him to find what needed to change so that he could be home more. I needed to know where he wanted this accountability to lead. After a few weeks of similar discussions, it became clear that while he said he wanted to be home earlier, it really wasn't important to him. At that point, we had to switch gears because I wasn't serving him in the most effective way.

Dr. Henry Cloud wrote a book called *The Power of the Other* about why accountability is so powerful. He says that without the power of another person, you're not taking advantage of accountability and therefore missing out on power and momentum in your life and business. Another person brings you to new heights, and without someone to hold you accountable, you'll be left in the dust.

A lot of people think successful business owners are arrogant and do not want to be accountable. People will not ask you if they can hold you accountable. The truth is not that owners are arrogant, but that being the leader is lonely. Employees, acquaintances, and even good friends can't relate to them, leading to a lot of superficial relationships. That is why people pay to get accountability from a coaching program. A lot of owners think accountability is messy and don't have the types of relationships that can handle it, so they hire a coach. As a coach, it's my job to care for my clients and make sure they do well. I want to invest in what they want.

People pick up on problems in different ways, and handle them differently, too. I'm a 2x4 person, just like a lot of owners tend to be. That means I may not see a problem in front of me until it smacks me in the face like a 2x4. A friend of mine is a toothpick person, though. He can't handle being hit with a problem that hard. He needs to have people bring it to his attention slowly, building the board with toothpicks a bit here and a bit there. In the end, though, everyone needs to say and hear hard things. The benefit of a coaching program is that I'll tell them what they *need* to hear. Employees tell owners what they *want* to hear—the information paints them in the best light. Way too many people tell owners that all of their ideas are great, but they're not. Rarely will someone push back, but a coach will. If you were a client and told me one of your goals was to meet more often with your sales team, my job is to call you out for only meeting with them once that month. I would also ask if that was still an important issue or if you wanted to focus on something else.

It's tough for a lot of people to get beyond embarrassment and benefit from an accountability partnership. You've got to admit weakness to someone and confess you can't do it alone. You're not weak, you're human. You may own a multi-million dollar company, but you've got to start admitting (at least to yourself, first) that there are areas for improvement in your work and personal life. Once you can be honest with yourself, tell someone else about your goals. When you do that, you're vulnerable, but it's so powerful. Owners tend to think they don't need help from anybody, but an accountability partner will accelerate your progress exponentially.

Don't start with lofty goals, and don't try to change everything you don't like about yourself at once. Start small and set specific, measurable benchmarks. If you tell someone that you want to eat better and take care of your body, they won't be able to tell if you're meeting your goal, especially if this is someone you see regularly. If you say you want to work out on an elliptical for 30 minutes five days a week, it's easy. Check "yes" or check "no," and when your accountability partner asks you about your progress, you'll know what to say. Both parties need to be committed. That doesn't mean your friend should show up at your house and drag you out of bed to workout. It just means you both need to be trustworthy and invested in success. If you have a prayer request, for example, a lot of people will tell you they will pray for you. Most of them will intend to, as well, but a lot will move on with their day and forget. You want an accountability partner who is going to be reliable enough to follow up. Coaches like myself are the people who follow up for a lot of business owners because it may not be safe to ask someone in their companies to hold them accountable. If you tell me three things you want to be held accountable for this month, we'll put a system in place to make sure it happens. It's safe, you will know what it looks like, and you'll know I will follow through.

I worked with the owner of a mortgage company once who had been on a quest for that silver-bullet salesperson. Since that person doesn't exist, he kept getting more frustrated with how his sales team was performing. As we talked, I realized there was no accountability in place for the sales team. You can hire the best people in the field, but they will not perform to your expectations if you don't hold them accountable.

This particular owner never got his team together for a meeting. The sales team was only six people, so I suggested getting them all around a table weekly. The purpose of the meetings would be to go over each salesperson's numbers from the previous week. However, no such data had ever been collected. The first person I had to hold accountable in this situation was the owner. We decided he needed to make a simple report, consisting of only "yes" or "no" questions, and have it ready for our next meeting.

When that was done, he had to figure out the best time in everyone's schedule for a weekly meeting. I coached him to get a consistent time on the calendar for the following three months. After he communicated the new expectations to his team and held them accountable, their performance skyrocketed. When salespeople see a peer performing better, they get competitive and want to be on top. Most employees naturally want to improve and be considered great at their jobs. Nobody wants to do poorly on a sales report. Knowing they would hear their teammates' results was a natural incentive to do well. Even if the boss never even commented on a poor report, people would know if they needed to step up their performance. This is an example of double accountability because it worked for the owner and the team. It would have been easy for the owner to dictate what his employees needed to do, but it never happened until we broke it down into manageable steps. Ultimately, I'd ask my client if he held the meetings that month, and eventually, they became sacrosanct at his office.

Another client I worked with had a much larger team. He had grown his business from the ground up and now had several hundred employees. He also had a leadership team with about 12 people. This owner increasingly felt that he was getting further out of touch with employees on the front lines every time the company grew. He used to know everybody, but couldn't possibly now. He wanted to have relationships with his employees because he felt that treating them well prevented them from looking for other jobs.

My job is to pull ideas out of clients. They do the dreaming, I fill in the blanks. This owner and I came up with the goal that he would have one-on-one meetings with each member of his leadership team once a month. That may not sound like a big deal, but time adds up. He needed to develop a structure to make this happen. We looked at his schedule and he decided to hold the meetings on Fridays. He would have three meetings every week.

You won't solve a big problem right away. Each step along the way is an opportunity for accountability. When the leadership team meetings were scheduled, then we came up with their format. During this step, he realized he needed to bring his assistant into the loop in order to prioritize this into the busy team's schedule. After establishing this routine, my client wanted each leadership team member to hold similar meetings with people in their departments. They learned from the boss and will now teach their team. This process trickled down into the organization and made more people feel connected. He accomplished his goal of connecting his employees, but each step was only possible through accountability.

"I'll do it when I get around to it" only becomes manageable when you ask someone else to join you in the process. That's what gives you the power to move from where you are to where you want to be. One step at a time gets you there a lot quicker.

CHAPTER 4
Health and Spirit

WE LIVE IN A WORLD THAT DOES NOT PRIORITIZE peace. We prioritize success, relationships, and happiness—all good things—but peace often falls by the wayside. Peace is internal and personal, not external. Therefore, people need to be intrinsically motivated to live peacefully. However, we live in a society that says we should be extrinsically motivated by wealth and material possessions, which trains us that the only way we can get what we want is to constantly be busy.

Peace is not a trophy. You can't tell people you have peace, but it is palpable to other people when you do, in fact, have it. Peace is not relational, but uniquely individual.

Yes, you can have peace in relationships, but peace does not rely on relationships. When we talk about a fulfilling life, we assume that there is peace. One huge part of fulfillment is having peace, but simply setting and achieving goals is not the same as having personal fulfillment.

We live in a world that does not prioritize peace

We buy into the belief that happiness is just around the corner. We will finally be happy when we have a good quarter, when we get a raise, when we land a major client, when the kids are back in school, when we pay off our loans, etc. However, as we have all learned by now, once we get there, a new obstacle to happiness pops up. So we continue on in the fruitless quest for happiness, convinced that if we just reach the horizon, success will be within our grasp. This natural tendency is the opposite of peace.

I'm not usually a big fan of referring to the dictionary, but I think the definition of peace is appropriate for the point I'm trying to make. Peace is defined as "freedom from disturbance; quiet and tranquility." You'll notice that this definition relies on circumstance; that is, if you are in a situation that is noisy or troublesome, you cannot have peace. Yet, we know that people can find peace even in the midst of personal tragedy, in the midst of a hectic schedule, or in the midst of the dull hum of everyday life.

If you are in a situation that is noisy or troublesome, you cannot have peace.

One of the most valuable aspects of inner peace is its consistency, its steadfastness even when times are tough. Peace is not defined by the absence of obstacles. Thus, there is peace beyond the dictionary definition.

Peace is completely internal; it is not dependent on circumstance. Success is external, but peace is not. It may be influenced by events in your life, but it is one of the few things completely within your control. So if we control whether we have peace, why do so few of us actually have peace? We simply do not prioritize it. Peace is a result of our thought life, which is something few of us learn to consciously control. Rather, we stumble along until we finally exhaust ourselves.

Our brain is powerful. We need to harness it instead of letting it control us. Since most people struggle with this concept, it's no surprise that most of my clients stare blankly at me when I bring it to their attention. They are used to hearing people say things like "stop being negative" or "fill your mind with positive thoughts," as if they can just wave a magic wand and it is done. That is complete nonsense, so let's get practical. Right off the bat, or right out of bed, you have to set the mood for the day. Saying positive affirmations to yourself is not off base here, so long as they are not hollow words. My staff thinks I'm crazy when I get to work, especially those who are not morning people, because as soon as I walk in the door, I tell everyone, "It's going to be a great day, we're going to make money, and we are going to love on people." I don't view it as crazy to set myself and my team up for positive expectations.

You've got to be purposeful about how you start your day or else your thoughts will take over. Too many of us fall into the trap of letting our to-do lists take over our thoughts before we get out of bed, sometimes before we even open their eyes. However, if you can retrain your brain and start your day by journaling, praying, or reading first thing in the morning, then your day will off to a much more purposeful start. No matter how you choose to start your day, try putting a positive message into your spirit before letting negative thoughts influence you.

Personally, I start my mornings by seeking the peace that comes from God. I can journal and read all I want, but I won't find the peace I need to start my day without quiet time with my heavenly father. I have to turn my whole spirit toward him because I want his to-do list to be mine. My clients may have different beliefs, though, so I encourage people to find their own routine.

> Too many of us fall into the trap of letting our to-do lists take over our thoughts before we get out of bed, sometimes before we even open their eyes.

With age comes wisdom. I believe that when it comes to peace, we learn as we go. When we get beyond our teenage angst and tumultuous twenties, we learn to live in a different way. This gradual improvement is not enough to protect our thought life, though. Without conscious effort, our minds will generally run amok. We quickly become unfocused and lose sight of what is important.

Most adults you know struggle to control their thought lives, which is why so many people experience a midlife crisis or get burnt out. This is a lesson so many of us have to learn the hard way. A trend I see is that this is happening to people at younger and younger ages. Even when people realize they are living this problem, they are not always successful in their attempt to be more peaceful. That is because peace is not something you achieve, it is something you believe.

Peace requires a different thought process than running a business. Success in business is not incompatible with peace, though. Peace doesn't require you to sell your belongings and live off the land. It doesn't require that you have every detail of your finances figured out over the next 20 years (although the financial planner in me recommends that you have some of the major aspects under control). Pursuing peace requires self-discipline to filter out distractions. So you have to ask yourself, what are the biggest things preventing you from experiencing peace? Take the opportunity to pause, reflect, and be honest with your answer to that question. For most of my clients, it's because they feel out of control. They feel like they are losing and not winning, which is sad. It may be common for owners to feel that way, but it is not normal, and it should not be your norm. If you own a successful business, I guarantee you that most people think your life is

> Success in business is not incompatible with peace.

a home run. That's why it bothers me when people think my clients are hitting it out of the park, yet they feel like losers.

Get back to the basics. You may already have everything you've ever wanted. Focus on that instead of the six things that are driving you nuts right now. The little things make a big difference. I like to see people be purposeful about that. In chapter one, we

> You may already have everything you've ever wanted. Focus on that instead of the six things that are driving you nuts right now.

discussed not going with the flow, because it will take you places you don't want to go. There will always be unhappy employees, bad decisions, missed deadlines, financial hits, and picky clients. You are going to have to deal with servers going down, people getting sick, and maybe even getting sued. Those are givens, if not constants, in business ownership. If you're not careful, any number of things can knock you off track on a daily basis.

Business owners have a lot of people grabbing at them. All of those people bring potential problems. Sell yourself right now on the idea that taking care of yourself is not selfish.

Doing what you love professionally can be addictive, and some owners view that as taking care of themselves. Getting the results you want and making money can be addictive, too. Entrepreneurs love the chase, they love the game. It is an intense, emotional journey. An unfortunate dark side of owning a business is not knowing a healthy way to take the edge off when pressure mounts and the lines between your work and personal life blur. The lows can send the strongest individuals sprawling, and we don't always resort to the healthiest coping mechanisms. Drugs and alcohol can quickly become a crutch. While temporary numbness masquerades as peace, it does not provide the long-term sense of wellness that peace does. In the long run, some habits become destructive. It is a lot easier to form a bad habit than a good one. Add in psychological predispositions, and things can easily become dicey.

Mental and Physical Health

Some of my coaching sessions bump up against mental health issues. It is common for my clients to just need someone who will listen, but sometimes it gets beyond that. I am not a mental health professional, and I know many people who swear that counseling works wonders. I always recommend seeking professional help because if you're no good to yourself, you're no good to any of the people who rely on you. I worked with the owner of a business valued at over $10 million, who was so frustrated and defeated that he was tempted to just give the company away. My job is to give clients perspective and faith for the future. If they aren't moving in a healthy direction after several attempts, I recommend professional help. A counselor always speeds up that process.

Business owners live an active and stressful life. They are constantly moving and on the go. Constantly moving and exercising are two different things, though. An essential part of exercise goes beyond the physical activity and affects your mental health. That's why when I have clients who aren't interested in working out because they don't feel like they need to lose weight, I push them to set fitness goals anyway.

If you haven't worked out in years, be realistic. Going from nothing to saying you're going to work out five days a week is setting yourself up for failure. You've got to get off the couch, though. Try taking a walk three times a week and incrementally add to your routine. Measure where you are now and set some goals without torturing your muscles. You're not going to lose 100 pounds this week, but you can get some endorphins flowing. If you decide to start walking, put it on your schedule. Otherwise, it's just a wish. There are so many great things that can come from a simple walk. It gives you a break to think during the day. If you go with your spouse, it can give you time to catch up without screens in front of you. If you choose to go by yourself, it will give your brain some much-needed silence.

> Try taking a walk three times a week and incrementally add to your routine.

Too many business owners skip their doctor's appointments, or worse, they don't schedule them at all. These visits get pushed to the sidelines. An excuse I frequently hear is, "they're just going to tell me to eat less

You need to have something in your life that gets you ***away from the business***, or it will constantly eat up 20 percent more of your time than you think.

and exercise more. I don't need to waste time on that!" While that may be part of a doctor's visit, they are also useful and can catch potential problems early. Even the act of preparing for a medical appointment involves paying extra attention to your body as you try to notice if there is anything you should discuss. Being in tune with your body is useful. Additionally, it takes away the "what if" worries. Instead of wondering whether something is problematic, you will either be reassured, or you will get it treated. People underestimate how beneficial that reassurance is for mental health. You wouldn't buy a Ferrari and refuse to take it in for scheduled maintenance.

We should do all we can to be good stewards of our health.

Health is so important to me because I've witnessed what can happen when a business owner neglects their own health. I made health an important part of my coaching business after I had a friend who was in the prime of his career drop dead of a heart attack. If you saw him, you wouldn't have noticed anything visibly unhealthy. He was in decent shape and didn't have any horrible habits, but I lived through the aftermath with his wife and their three daughters for the next 15 years.

We should do all we can to be good stewards of our health. One of the first questions I ask a client is about his or her health and about the last time they went to see a doctor. Owners have a lot of people who count on them, and the best thing you can do for those people is to take care of yourself. When you're on an airplane, they instruct you to put on your oxygen mask first in the case of an emergency. That way, you can be there to put on your children's mask. If you don't help yourself first, who will be there to help them?

My friend's wife had been telling him, "let us take care of you" for years, but hearing that didn't work for him. Like a lot of owners, being responsible for others was a part of who he was. Unfortunately, a lot of owners put themselves last. He worked in the healthcare industry and lived in a community that was underserved in that area. He viewed taking care of himself as taking resources from the community. He didn't realize that taking care of himself meant that he would be around to provide resources to those who needed them in the future.

> Unfortunately, a lot of owners put themselves last.

Lead yourself first

If you've owned your business for 20 years, then you've been putting others first for 20 years. People think this is being selfless, but it can get you out of whack if you only think about today and not the long game. Take care of your brain, spirit, and body, because this is the one tool you have. Like any craftsman, you've got to take care of your tool. For whatever reason, American and entrepreneurial culture doesn't think this way. Owners take on a lot for a lot of people. There is a good quality there, but it's like a pendulum, and it can swing too far in one direction.

You need to have something in your life that gets you away from the business, or it will constantly eat up 20 percent more of your time than you think. A lot of owners think they have outside interests, but a surprising number of their hobbies are really just opportunities to network. Even altruistic groups, such as the Rotary Club, quickly turn into creating relationships for the sake of connections. Truly "selfish" outside interests are key—the more impractical, the better. Think anti productivity. For me, it's church, because my faith is critical to my peace. Whatever that thing is for you, it's helpful to spend time with people who share your core beliefs. There's something about the combination of ritual and spirituality that is valuable to many people, including myself.

> A lot of owners think they have outside interests, but a surprising number of their hobbies are really just opportunities to network.

Volunteering can be rewarding, too. While some owners think offering pro bono services counts as volunteering, it does not provide an escape from the office. Finding ways to serve is easy. In most communities, you can find everything from one-day service groups to organizations dedicated to a specific cause every week. You might serve dinner at a homeless shelter, pull weeds at the community garden, or pass out water at a charity run. Sometimes the most mindless work often provides the greatest benefits. I have found laying bricks to be surprisingly peaceful. In addition, sharing an experience with others is inherently beneficial. Whether you tutor children, serve in Sunday school, do yard work, or clean the streets, volunteering is an outlet that pays off not only for you, but for your community.

Investing time on an outside interest is the key. It can be as simple as joining a book club or playing cards. I've had clients take up ballroom dancing because it gives them the same outlet with the benefit of spending time with their spouse. Spending too much time on any one thing creates imbalance. It's not healthy or sustainable in the long haul if all you have is your business.

> Spending too much time on any one thing creates imbalance.

A hobby frees up your creativity. Owners sometimes think it's selfish to focus on themselves, but everyone is happier when the boss is happy. Like we talked about previously, if you're always busy, you're not always busy doing the right thing or giving your time to the highest and best use.

Peaceful transformations

In One-Life Game Plan™ coaching sessions, we don't have preconceived notions about what every owner needs. My job is to get to know you and then assess your needs since the program is about the whole individual, not just their business, and not just checking boxes. Your job is to be honest about what you want. I'll ask some questions, and through that process, the client decides what's right for him or her. Sessions and goals will look totally different for every person. My mission is to keep moving my clients forward, no matter if they start at the top of Mount Everest or at base camp. After all, peace is relative, it's not a nirvana place.

One of my clients struggled with a lack of peace when he decided he didn't want to miss seeing his three young children grow up anymore. He made a commitment to his family that he would stop working 70 hours a week and top out at 50. After that, he decided not to look at his phone at night and set his work email to "do not disturb" mode from 6 p.m. to 6 a.m. This allowed him to be more present with his kids. A few years later, he said that difference was priceless. He couldn't put a value on how spending time with his kids improved their relationships and his level of peace.

Talk therapy to deal with anxiety

Running a business produces a lot of anxiety. Another client of mine recently lost her mother, had a rocky relationship with her business partner, and had been losing money at work. During the One-Life process, it occurred to her that she should reconnect with her therapist to work on her mental health. A lot of research points to how effective talk therapy is at bringing down anxiety. Something that

Organizations have plans and budgets because they realize *there are only so many things they can accomplish in 12 months.*

had been holding her down was the cost, but her personal peace was worth the investment.

Sometimes you just have to try something new, too. When I was working with someone going through health problems, I asked him if he had any kind of workout routine. He said "no," and added that he had put on 40 pounds over the years. He tried a few different things before he discovered how much he loved CrossFit. Pulling ropes and flipping tires is not for everyone, but he really enjoyed it because of the variety of exercises. He jumped in headfirst and started putting it on his calendar regularly. Right away it gave him more energy, which was great because he had complained about feeling beat up all the time. Now that he's been working out for several years, his weight is down, he looks great, and his stress levels have decreased.

There was a surgeon that I used to work with who had been at the top of his field. He was one of the hardest-working people in medicine, so he was constantly busy and viewed that as a positive thing. Then, at age 43, he had to stop operating when he was diagnosed with stage-four colon cancer. After going through different rounds of surgery and therapy, he went back to work part-time. While he couldn't operate, he could still see patients. Not too long after he started working again, he experienced his "aha" moment and realized what he had been doing wrong his whole career. Not only did he regret all the hours, but he used to go into the office and barely acknowledge the staff. Now, he actually cared and wanted to get to know them. He needed to slow down in order to realize he wasn't taking care of himself or others.

There is something to be learned from slowing down and quieting your mind. Some call it meditating, but that word scares a lot of people because they don't understand it. I've seen it work for a lot of clients, though. Taking care of your spirit is a big deal. We're our own worst critics, and we feel like we have to be great at everything we do. We've got to be great owners, parents, community members, and everything else. That's why the U.S. is No. 1 in a lot of business categories: we strive for innovation and greatness.

Sometimes we get things upside down, though. If you're going to spend 18 hours a day awake, take the first hour (or even half an hour, really) to think about what you want to happen that day. Think of a large organization. It's not going to just start the fiscal year and magically do great things. Organizations have plans and budgets because they realize there are only so many things they can accomplish in 12 months. That's why they focus on doing the most important things and not just doing things. Imagine if you could start each day with that level of strategic planning.

It's not that business owners don't want to be doers, it's that they focus too much on that role in their lives. Being a business owner may be part of who you are, but it is not *all* of who you are. If you seek the satisfaction of knowing that things are going in the right direction (your relationships, family, goals you have outside of work, *and* your business), then you must use the first hour of your day to examine who you are and what you want to accomplish. Everyone has a long to-do list. Retrain your mind to check off eight items every day in hopes that your highest-priority items reach desirable outcomes.

A nudge to reprioritize

In our One-Life program, we nudge people to reprioritize, but we don't force it. You have to want to understand yourself; that's what our game plan is all about. Having a successful life is more than how much money you can make, what you spend it on, and who you impress. It's about living according to what matters to you. Whatever you value, live like those things are important to you instead of just letting life happen. Henry David Thoreau said it best in *Walden,*

> *"The mass of men lead lives of quiet desperation. ... But it is a characteristic of wisdom not to do desperate things."*

Personally, I start most of my days quietly reflecting on what's important to me. Am I putting those things first? Am I listening to God? Am I taking care of my wife and watching out for her spirit, too? My business is important, but it's not in the top three on my list. I found that taking walks in the mornings helps me reflect. There is a prayer garden not far from my office that is my go-to destination when the weather cooperates.

Health and spirit go hand in hand

If your spirit is not nurtured, then everything else gets out of whack. Your health will deteriorate, or it may seem to be the case. I coached a client who was in perfect shape. Amateur bodybuilding was a hobby for him. He worked out all the time, fueled his body with a healthy diet, and it showed. One day he told me about a lump that had been on his neck for a while. He had noticed it two years earlier but was crippled by fear about what the doctor might tell him. When he finally had it checked out, it turned out to be a benign cyst, yet for two years, he held on to the anxiety that he may be dying. He felt like his health was failing, and it clouded everything else. A man who has his health has a million dreams; a man who doesn't have his health only has one.

Don't wait, start now.

Sometimes people don't know where to start when I explain the importance of a healthy spirit. I encourage them to journal. Don't wait, start now. Take stock of where you are in five areas: spiritually, physically, intellectually, emotionally, and socially. I call these my five "tanks." This is a common model, but it helps to start here and build the habit. That way, if you really don't have time to journal every day, you can reflect in your head no matter where you are. I've been stuck in traffic and reflected on these areas. If one or more of your tanks is low, you can make decisions to help yourself even when you get busy.

Buck Jacobs, author, founder, and chairman of The C12 Group, said, "priorities are what we do, everything else is just talk." You can say all you want about your commitment to wellness, but if your schedule looks like a roadmap to disaster, then you are lying to yourself. You have to prioritize not only your personal relationships, but also yourself. Being selectively selfish is necessary.

Make peace a priority. Walk your dog. Do yoga. Eat breakfast at the table for a change instead of in your car. Create a new ritual. Forming better habits requires discipline, even when that habit is something we think we should succeed in naturally.

CHAPTER 5
Sales Process

You don't have to be a business professor to know that everything comes down to sales. This is a big area in an owner's life, obviously. It's also fraught with problems because most owners do not even have a sales process. In large part, this is because they either came up through sales or developed sales skills over the years. In One-Life Game Plan™ sessions, we view this as a high-leverage area. Where can we exert the least amount of pressure to move the biggest rock? The sales process.

The vast majority of owners have a sales mindset. There are two major mistakes owners make when it comes to having a sales process, though. They either rely too much on themselves as the top-producing salesperson, or they put this weight on a single salesperson. I can't stress enough that the silver bullet salesman that every owner looks for does not exist. Yet, a lot of companies out there try to sell owners on the idea that if they pay X amount of dollars for a person or method, then their sales problems will be solved. The problem with buying into a program like this is that it usually only produces one person, and you have to teach that process to other people if you want your business to be scalable. Another common problem is that owners who have already assembled a team tend to look for a sales manager. They want someone with the perfect amount of experience that can solve their problems.

> There is nothing magical about a single person or program.

The reality is there is nothing magical about a single person or program. It's about basic sales blocking and tackling, processes and procedures. Owners just want to write a check and get that person, program, or secret to be their solution. Unfortunately, success in sales is a mystery to some people, so they forget it's about basic systems just like any other part of business. Because sales involves people with influence, owners may think a great salesperson is just born with that natural talent. I don't believe a great salesperson is born, I believe salespeople can be trained.

Your sales process doesn't have to be complex. Some companies start out with a series of scripts or videos about how to sell a product. Every product is unique, so every sales

THE "SILVER BULLET SALESMAN" THAT EVERY OWNER LOOKS FOR DOES NOT EXIST.

process is unique, and so is the follow-through. Owners need to constantly go through scenarios and role-play the scripts with their team. The secret is not magic, it's having a process to begin with. If you want to scale, you've got to get something down on paper. Anyone can be 80-percent as good as the "natural born" salesman if they start with a process. No matter if you have one or 50 people on your team, that's your starting line. Some owners want to hire a manager first and then come up with the process,

> Anyone can be 80-percent as good as the "natural born" salesman if they start with a process.

but that's foolish. Get the process first, but if you already have a team, there's no time to lose. The sales process is one of the first areas of the business we talk about in One-Life Game Plan™ sessions because it's crucial to the success of the company.

When I ask clients if they have a written sales process, answers go from "kind of" to "not really" pretty quickly. Then they get around to asking me, "what's the big deal if I don't have one?" After all, they started out as the sole salesperson and learned through trial by fire and making mistakes, so why can't others? That's flawed logic. Owners aren't fully aware of how they taught themselves until I point it out. They benefited from being naturally aware of their own ideal customer. Not only did they learn general sales skills, but also how to sell their own business—a unique and specific skill set that can be summarized in a set of processes. The problem is that most owners have not created this summary process. When they hire salespeople or a sales manager, they hire for general sales skills and then fail to pass on the knowledge of the process.

Once again, a client may say, "but I learned without any knowledge of a sales process, and I picked it up on the job." However, you had an intimate connection with other parts of the business from the time you started. You lived and died by QuickBooks. As the owner, you had a unique insight into the relationship between your sales process and your bottom line. You saw how it played out in real-time and were privy to all the details. You had a unique viewpoint because you saw how the sales process fits into the larger scope of the business. Your next sales manager is not going to see this side of the business with such depth. He or she will have a much more limited scope.

> It is impossible to grasp the importance of sales metrics without understanding the sales process.

It is impossible to grasp the importance of sales metrics without understanding the sales process. In other words, when owners sell, they understand the "why" of sales without assistance, but sales managers need the "why."

Your sales manager does not—and never will—have your high-level perspective of how sales affects the business. No matter how dedicated, talented, or intelligent, even given time, he or she will not learn the process in the same way you did. It's up to you—the owner—to convey this process. This is not because you're some sort of sales wizard, but because you have access to the big picture.

Process makes perfect

To ensure success, create a system that allows someone with a narrower view to use his or her strengths to win the game. If you can explain this to someone else, then they can now take an analytical look at the sales process and offer ways to improve it. The existence and explanation of the process enables you and your managers to make the improvements. This lets people who are better at sales than you into the system. It sets them up for success. So even if you already have salespeople who are better at sales than you, it is still necessary to set up the process. In chapter three, we discussed how many employees don't know what a good day looks like in their position because they don't have relevant key performance indicators. The first sales manager at a company often fails because he or she is thrown into an environment where there is not a system in place.

As an owner, you have the ability tot meet potential prospects and immediately know what questions to ask. You know your ideal client, and you know exactly how far from that ideal client you are willing to stray. Put a salesperson in that position, and even the most talented people will base the conversation on how comfortable they feel in their career rather than how good of a fit the client is for the business. A "green" sales representative will chat them

> You know your ideal client, and you know exactly how far from that ideal client you are willing to stray.

up briefly and make a snap decision based largely on whether they have already met their sales goals for the quarter. More seasoned salespeople will be pickier, not because they have learned what is best for the business, but because they have learned what is best for their careers. They know how to meet the performance indicators they established for themselves independent from the KPIs set by the company. Salespeople fall back on methods like these when they don't have clear performance goals and metrics. This is why it is so important that owners communicate to sales managers what needs to happen—so that their team's KPIs match what the business needs. If there is a disconnect, you will experience problems throughout the sales process. This illustrates the key point: the direction of salespeople does not automatically match the direction of the business. It is up to owners and sales managers to define that direction. The system is the key to keeping the two together at all times. Otherwise, they will naturally stray from one another.

> Owners must communicate to sales managers what needs to happen—so that their team's KPIs match what the business needs.

It's not that a sales process is difficult to teach, or even that owners are poor teachers, but that owners don't see the value of a process in general. They can get so bogged down in the day-to-day logistics of running a company, which is why they see the need to go after the next big client without a process as more immediate than taking the time to formulate the process. Documenting the sales process is not difficult, time-consuming, or mystical. Owners spend more time intimidated by the idea of writing it than it would take to put it on paper. Focus on writing out the process, not on the process being perfect. You're not writing a final draft, but the first of many. This will allow you to more clearly see some of the small things that need to be fixed so that your sales team will produce great results down the road.

I'll concede that companies can grow and be successful without a sales process. My clients are all successful owners before they even sit down with me, yet the majority don't have these systems in place. This is because their success is largely due to their own gifting and passion, coupled with the luck of starting with other gifted individuals. While their accomplishments are already amazing, those gifts can only take a company so far, but they cannot grow it to scale.

> Focus on writing out the process, not on the process being perfect.

We've discussed the type of owners who start as the top salesperson and have difficulty letting go, but there are also the owners that become out of touch with the sales department. These are the owners who struggle to write a sales process because they don't know how their salespeople spend half of their time. This reminds me of a famous quote from department store magnate John Wanamaker, who said, "half the money I spend on advertising is wasted; the trouble is, I don't know which half."

This type of owner needs to be reminded that what can be measured can be managed. Owners need to know that is a truism and that there are practical steps they can take. Start with the top 20 percent of your company's sales. Analyze them, go through them individually to find what they have in common. Figure out why the top 20 percent of your clients are doing business with you. Then figure out how to duplicate that type of business. Does this top tier come from the same industry? What unique needs do they have that your company is so great at serving? Take those findings and build them into your sales process. This needs to be in place before you look to grow your sales team or hire a manager.

Hiring a sales manager

Many clients have asked me for advice on hiring a sales manager, and it's tough. You've got to want to hire someone for the right reasons. They won't magically fix all of your problems. Make sure you have realistic expectations for this hire so you don't waste time and money training someone who won't work out. If you hire someone based on his or her success with another company, that doesn't mean they'll see similar success without breaking stride. If you promote a successful salesperson, that does not mean they will be a successful sales manager. Having the sales process in place will definitely increase your batting average when it comes to hiring employees who stick around.

When it comes to hiring sales staff, I advise owners to be slow to hire and fast to fire. What you're looking for is a hard worker who likes people and likes to be helpful. Hire someone who is competitive but not too competitive or self-centered. You want a team player, of course, because you're looking to scale.

There are some characteristics to avoid, too. You don't want someone if they're not focused on metrics. If a potential candidate tells you they can do 10 things well, ask them how they measure their outcomes. You want someone who can explain what they do and why it's effective. Otherwise, they'll waste any money you budget for them. Get someone who is focused so that if they have a $300,000 budget, they'll spend it on what works.

> Be slow to hire and fast to fire.

Step 1: Create a sales funnel

The first step to hiring a sales manager is creating a sales funnel. This is a visual representation of where different clients are in the sales process, from the broadest function—you have classified them as potential clients but not contacted them—to the follow-up stage. This creates structure. This is the "glue" that holds the salesperson's and business's goals together. We'll talk about this more in-depth in the next chapter covering operational levers, but for now, consider this step one.

Step 2: Schedule consistent face-to-face meetings

Step two is scheduling regular face-to-face sales meetings. I've mentioned how few companies actually get their sales team around a table on a regular basis, and it always baffles me because it is an easy way to naturally spark the competitive nature of salespeople. These meetings, in addition to your sales funnel, help the team to identify KPIs, giving them a concrete organizational system. Every lead can then be classified into one of a few categories rather than seeing each lead as somewhere between a potential customer and a paying customer. Once this system is in place, it becomes easier to set performance goals because the group of leads is broken down into manageable categories.

Establishing these KPIs is only half the battle, though. Keeping performance on track is still an issue. Meetings keep people accountable and give managers the opportunity to reset the course, if necessary. Tracking is half the battle. Providing accountability is key. Establishing direction is critical, and now

Schedule **consistent** face-to-face meetings.

that it's in place, you have to stay the course. This requires consistent check-ins to ensure everyone is staying on the established path. It reinforces a salesperson's KPIs, which goes back to the clarity of expectations we discussed in chapter two.

What is your market?

That's the key question to ask yourself. Most small to midsize businesses don't target enough customers. They can't afford to compete in marketing and advertising with large companies for brain time. Corporations such as Apple, Amazon, and McDonald's inundate the populous with their marketing messages.

A smaller market is better. The type of owner I work with does not run (and does not want to run) a Walmart-style business, relying on small margins to entice customers. The smaller your market is, the less competition you have, which means you have more freedom in your pricing strategies. You've probably heard of Renée Mauborgne and W. Chan Kim's book *Blue Ocean Strategy: How to Create Uncontested Market Space and Make the Competition Irrelevant*. This book became an instant classic when it came out in 2004, and I wholeheartedly recommend reading it. It defends the idea of getting away from competitors and creating new markets in much more details than I can write in this chapter. For small and midsize business owners, the Blue Ocean strategy necessitates almost a niche market. While this can be difficult, you have to remember that you can't please everyone. You can only provide the maximum value to a relatively small market segment, no matter what industry you are in. This strategy requires owners to think differently

> Most small to midsize businesses don't target enough customers.

and take their company to a market where nobody else exists.

The book's title refers to the metaphor that when there are too many sharks feeding in the same space, the ocean becomes red from the carnage. In the business world, when everyone is doing the popular thing, the space becomes so murky and hard to navigate that it's almost impossible for a company to thrive. Some businesses just exist on what's available without opportunities for growth or innovation.

When a company adopts the Blue Ocean strategy, they are making the decision not to compete anymore but to find a new ocean without sharks. There are so many great examples of this, and I have worked with a couple of business owners who were already successful, took the Blue Ocean approach, and saw unprecedented results.

> Some businesses just exist on what's available without opportunities for growth or innovation.

> Create a list, and keep it updated.

An innovative approach to medicine

One client ran a successful internal medicine practice. The office had been around for a long time, competing with countless others for the same patients. He starting wondering what could set his practice apart, and it occurred to him that the universal complaint patients have about any medical practice is the waiting room. Nobody wants to waste their time sitting around, especially when they are not feeling well and have to be near other sick patients. So, he came up with this idea of a concierge practice. His patients would pay a flat—and handsome—rate for the year, can visit his office as much as they need to, and have full access to their doctor via phone and email. This not only resolved the top complaint of patients but the top complaint of doctors: dealing with insurance. If he charged a flat amount to a certain amount of clients, he wouldn't have to deal with insurance companies to get paid. Even better, it would allow him to have a smaller caseload of patients. This was a brand new concept, and people who wanted something different were willing to pay for it. Now, it's certainly not for everyone. Most people who have decent medical insurance through their employers would not want to pay to see this doctor. However, he was able to sign up enough patients who saw value in this type of doctor-patient relationship.

An innovative computer support company

Another example of an owner who created a new space in a traditional industry owned a computer support company. Typically, a midsize company would have to hire a full-time IT employee. That's a large salary, plus benefits, for some to basically be an insurance policy against crashing computers. Technology is already expensive, plus it is constantly changing. If you have 75 computers, on any given day you don't know if you're going to have 10 problems or 1,000. Some days that employee doesn't have much work to do, and on other days they need help. So, someone came up with the idea of charging companies a fixed rate to be their on-call IT team. Customers would have their technology needs met and wouldn't have to have any IT staff on payroll. No matter how many computer issues a client had that day, the remote IT team would have the ability to provide support immediately. These IT services are more common, but it's an example of how someone thought differently and created a market where none existed.

Starting the process

Whether you know it or not, there is already a sales process in place in your business. If like many owners, you don't have it written down, then your sales process is probably pretty simple. Your team is likely identifying potential clients, sporadically contacting them, and waiting to hear back. You will get some new business this way— people who are in desperate need of your services will become your customers. People who either want your services or don't know they need your services will disappear early on when this process prevails, though. Ultimately, these two huge categories of prospective customers—the wants and the don't-know-they-needs—can provide you with more sales than you can handle. However, they are not going to fall into your lap. In order to access these sources of customers, you need to go out and get them. You already have an idea of how to get more customers, but there must be a system in place. Otherwise, you can only access a tiny fraction of the individuals or businesses you could be reaching.

Structure is key to managing anyone, but especially a sales team. Set a direction for them as employees to ensure that their success and the company's success are intertwined. When people are dealing with complex processes, it is necessary to have a system in place to keep things organized. Sales is an extremely complex process. There are countless unknowns, and it is necessary to adapt to endless permutations. Even a salesperson with a single prospect has his or her hands full because the sales process has a wide variety of unpredictable possible outcomes at every stage. When salespeople have multiple prospects, this becomes unmanageable. Left to fate, those who are desperate will become customers, and those who are not will drift off into the distance, never to be seen again.

Your first sales process draft should include every step from the top to the bottom of your sales funnel. Once you have this written down, you can come up with a formula. For example, one of our clients uses something like this:

10	touches
= 4	in-person meetings
= 1	new client

The power to estimate how your different sales tactics will pay off is invaluable. In addition, once you get a formula, you can start trying to tweak it. If you start narrowing your targeting, do you see fewer touches getting the same number of in-person meetings? If you change your meetings, do you see the number of clients go up or down? This is key to tracking how changing your processes influences the number of new clients.

Integrating technology

Start by tracking your leads. Step one is monitoring your contacts. Who have you spoken to? Who should you be reaching out to? Create a list, and keep it updated. There are several automated customer relationship management (CRM) systems that integrate sales and marketing, such as Infusionsoft or HubSpot. These tools can be incredibly effective and take a great deal of pressure off of you and your sales team. If you opt to use an automated system, it does require a dedicated person on your team to take on these responsibilities. Don't invest in training an employee unless you plan on keeping him or her around or believe you can easily find someone else with familiarity with the platform.

Technology is an increasingly important part of the sales process. Make sure you have a plan to integrate a variety of marketing tools.

Since the sheer number of technology options any owner has can be overwhelming, I've included a short list of four things to consider in your plan:

1. Your website

If your domain has nothing else, it should provide a way to contact you. It sounds obvious, but this should be front and center. Potential clients will take their business elsewhere if they have to click around too much to find your information. In addition, think of your website as a pre-qualifier. Your site should encourage your ideal prospects to contact you by appealing to them, specifically and directly. Your site does not need to be all things to all people—its job is to court your top prospects.

2. Outgoing email program

Automating this system is one of the easiest ways to keep in touch with prospects.

3. Outdoor advertising

Signage is often overlooked, but this can be a great way to market your company. Outdoor advertising is increasingly different, especially these days. It sets you apart from the competition, which should be your goal.

4. Networking

Trade groups, conferences, and other events that bring people together are invaluable. Many groups are holding more virtual network events to make it easier for more people to attend. However, nothing beats face-to-face interaction. Conferences give you the ability to make connections in real-time, which is a rarity now. I find that most business owners are fairly diligent about pursuing networking opportunities for themselves, but they forget about their staff. It may be useful to suggest networking events for your salespeople. If you have had success at a particular event over the years, consider sending a sales manager or senior salesperson. Setting your people up for success, as opposed to taking on the work yourself, is more sustainable for your business. In addition, salespeople do not have the same demands on their time; they can really shine in the follow-up process after the event. You might take a week or two to respond to individuals you met, but your salespeople can prioritize the lead-nurturing process.

These tools can be incredibly effective and take a great deal of pressure off of you and your sales team.

The sales process

We've talked about it, you've read examples, now let's get to work. I'd like to fully break down the sales process for you. Keep in mind that there is as much diversity in sales processes as in the business community, but there are some universal truths and best practices that can go into every sales process. Whether you are a sales expert or a reluctant salesperson, here are the steps you should have in place (first for yourself, and then for your sales manager).

❶ Incoming inquiry form

This can be tailored to your website, email, phone system, or any type of technology or method you use for incoming leads. Whatever information you receive from leads in their inquiry, make sure you keep it updated and organized. There is a CRM a lot of my clients use called Insightly for this type of contact. Put that information in whatever system you are using to track your contacts, and put it in whatever you use to track your sales funnel, such as Infusionsoft. This data is useless to you unless it is in your CRM.

❷ Email needs-requirement diagnostic form

I encourage my clients to invest a substantial amount of time developing a needs-requirement form. You want to get as much relevant information as possible from the potential customer without making the form too long. There are two main issues to keep in mind with these forms:

Ask for the right information

This requires you to know the definition of an ideal client. Start by looking at the top tier of your existing clients. These are the clients you can provide superior value to and who appreciate you in return. Look for commonalities across this group. A good place to start is annual income. In addition, look at who your hypothetical ideal client would be. This may enlighten you as to what your target market should be. Keep in mind that this form is something that can be tweaked. You will need to adjust the questions as you go. This is why having a sales process is so critical: you can identify problems that are common to a particular level in the sales funnel.

Ask the questions in the right way

Your clients expect you to know the technical jargon, but they don't have the time or the desire to learn it themselves. Therefore, watch out for places where it is unclear what information you may be asking them to provide.

❸ Review the diagnostic form for the proper fit

This is where you identify qualified leads, separating the wheat from the chaff. Particularly for creative agencies, it is crucial to choose carefully here since proposals can often be costly in time. I encourage my clients not to provide spec work since that does not reflect the actual value of their services. When you are looking for a proper fit, there are two major questions to consider:

Do the customers' needs align with your strengths?

If the customer is looking for services that you can provide but that you probably shouldn't, then it is best to let them go. At this point in the process, you should be able to identify these types of prospects fairly easily. If you find that unsuitable clients are getting too far down the sales funnel, you need to review your diagnostic form and make changes to try to qualify leads in a more concrete way.

Can you estimate that the scope aligns with your ideal work?

For example, if you are a mid-sized digital marketing agency fielding an inquiry from a local restaurant that is looking to tweak their existing website, you would likely find that the scope of the project is too small.

❹ Redirect customers that don't fit

If a prospect doesn't work out based on the answers to the questions above, redirect them. You should have a variety of smaller and larger firms who target people across a variety of industries. By setting up leads that aren't viable for you with companies that can provide them with value, you work toward becoming a trusted referral source for the other companies, and you also manage to keep a valuable contact.

❺ Diagnostic meeting

If the prospect is a proper fit, schedule a diagnostic meeting. You will have a limited amount of time, so you need to know what information you need to get from them. Outline these needs and the project scope with the client team.

❻ Budget buy-in

It is critical at this point to get buy-in on the project budget from the client. Notice that the budget buy-in takes place relatively early in the process. Too often, people put this off for a variety of reasons. Owners and salespeople might want to avoid an uncomfortable conversation. The creative team might be off to the races and too excited about the project to get bogged down in the details. You may even have a project management problem and be unsure who is responsible for getting the budget buy-in from the client. Whatever the reason, it is critical to broach this issue early on. Qualifying your lead is not enough. The prospective client might be willing to agree to the budget and scope in theory, but in practice, it may be a different story. This gap between theory and practice is why budgetary issues can be ongoing throughout the sales process. You don't want to finish the project or put in a lot of work and have the client dispute the bill. If you get buy-in at this stage, before the work is started, you are much less likely to run into post-project disputes. In addition, when you have documentation outlining this information for your clients, then you will have a much easier time addressing any issues when they do arise.

❼ Deliver the proposal

Put the scope of the work in writing and get it to the client. This is your formal written proposal that encompasses your plan for the entire project.

❽ Agree on the timeline

This is just as important as the budget so that the project doesn't run over on your end. Get out the calendar and have these discussions with the client. Make sure to put scarcity in the process.

⑨ Sign the agreement

Have the client sign a document that includes the payment schedule and initial payment. Sound obvious? Unfortunately, businesses regularly lose money at this stage. Make sure you do not approve of any work to begin before receiving the initial payment.

⑩ Ask for referrals

Don't hesitate to ask the client who else your sales team should be talking to. Yes, it is OK to be direct in asking for referrals.

⑪ Start working

I realize this is step 11. You may be reading this and thinking, "this is overkill." Well, in a sense, it is overkill. I would not recommend that a start-up or brand new business use these steps. This sales process is meant for an established business with enough breathing room to take the time to do things correctly and hire sales professionals who can get results.

⑫ Follow up

Depending on the type of work you do, you may or may not come into contact with the client frequently while the work is going on. That's why it is important to be proactive in keeping in touch with the client.

CHAPTER 6
Operational Levers

WHAT IS AN OPERATIONAL LEVER? That is the question I get all the time when I introduce this concept to clients. Simply put, this is where money is made—or not made—in most businesses. However, maybe it's easier to start by explaining what an operational lever is not. Not every opportunity for decreasing costs is an operational lever.

Remember "counting pencils"? Business owners tend to get caught up in the small details—areas that are likely best delegated to someone else and do not significantly affect profitability. Some spend a disproportionate amount of time trying to save on small costs, such as office supplies, rather than trying to increase efficiency in some of the most expensive areas of the business. Here's another example: when an owner tries to save on janitorial costs by cleaning the office themselves. Sure, they save a few dollars, but at what cost? Missing the kids' games on the weekends, family dinners, or a chance to sit down and plan for next quarter? It's not worth your time to clean the office, and it rarely turns out as well as it would have if a professional had taken care of the job. Owners just don't usually know how to get those streak-free windows.

These small costs are not worth getting bogged down over. Yet over and over, I see owners making the same types of mistakes, no matter what industry they are in. This is a really ineffective way to cut costs, and it's definitely not a way to improve profitability. Now that we have explained what an operational lever is not, let's return to the question at the beginning of the chapter. What is an operational lever?

What is an operational lever?

Operational levers are areas of your business that have the biggest impact on profitability while making the least effort. You may not remember much of your high school physics class, but you certainly have used a lever before. The concept is pretty simple: placing a bar across a fulcrum, you vary the distance between the fulcrum and whatever you're trying to move in order to make it easier to move the object.

Think about how much time and effort you have spent trying to reduce costs in areas of your business like web hosting for your own company site, saving on office supplies, or not replacing items such as printers and computer monitors. There are two reasons these are not operational levers. First, they are relatively small costs—you can find web hosting for as little as $10 per month. Paperclips tend to be pretty cheap, too, unless you buy them individually.

Frequency is key to understanding operational levers.

The second reason is that they are not frequently repeated costs. They appear monthly, quarterly, or even yearly, so the savings don't quickly accrue. If you own a digital agency, though, that has a high volume of websites, then web hosting may be an operational lever. That is a repeated cost. However, if you have a small accounting firm, your own site's web hosting is not an operational lever.

While there tend to be similarities within specific industries, your business model determines your operational levers. For example, most digital agencies have substantial payroll costs. However, some agencies frequently respond to *requests for proposals* (RFPs). Some occasionally respond, and some avoid the RFP process altogether. That means that for some agencies, the RFP process may be an operational lever. However, others may not use that method frequently enough to make it an operational lever. Operational costs are variable costs, rather than fixed costs, but not all variable costs are operational levers, either. The cost must be significant enough *and* repeat enough to be an operational lever.

Since operational levers are by definition repeated frequently, even small increases in efficiency can be duplicated so often that they become large increases in profit. Similarly, small errors in these areas have substantial costs for a business. Frequency is key to understanding operational levers. Remember this: an increase in efficiency corresponds to a decrease in the error rate. Simply doing things faster does not necessarily increase efficiency.

An increase in efficiency corresponds to a decrease in the error rate. Simply doing things faster does not necessarily increase efficiency.

Operational levers and your people

One of our clients owns a heavy equipment repair shop. While the business was growing, the owner came to us looking to improve profit. We decided to work together to determine what the operational levers were and how to use that information to make small changes where they would have the greatest possible impact.

We started by looking at the revenue function, and one of the first things we noticed was a variance between the actual time per job and the labor time quoted. For an engine overhaul, the quotes estimated the time at 21 hours.

However, the actual time spent varied between 25 and 35 hours—up to 67 percent longer than the estimate. There are two reasons this is an operational lever for this business. First, this is a variable cost. Every single job required a quote and actual labor (variable cost as opposed to fixed costs, such as rent or other costs that do not increase or decrease based on units sold). Next, engine overhauls happened to be a fairly common job, so this small mistake was repeated over and over again.

Payroll was this shop's biggest expense. To put it in perspective, the next most expensive cost category was 25 percent of payroll costs. You can clearly see that labor represents a hugely important resource for this company. Another thing to consider is that payroll is paid in cash, and it's not possible to defer these costs. This indicates that the first place to improve efficiency is in the category of labor. Changes in this area will have the greatest impact.

> Once we identified the lever, we had to change the system.

It is important to note that the problem was not necessarily that the engine overhauls were taking too long. The problem was the discrepancy between actual time and quoted time. Once we identified the lever, we had to change the system to ensure that the quoted labor time was at least equal to the actual labor time. In this case, the issue was with a lack of training. With no training in this area, technicians had no way to gauge whether the job was on schedule. All technicians need proper front-end information (i.e., everyone should know that an engine overhaul should take 21 hours).

Once again, you can see why the holistic approach that the One-Life Game Plan™ takes is necessary. In this case, the operational lever was directly related to the technicians' lack of relevant KPIs on the project level (how many hours the job should take), which is a topic we covered in chapter two.

Operational levers are key for scaling your business

We identified another operational lever when a client who owned a growing medical practice was looking to increase profit. Both of the clients we've discussed in this chapter so far faced a similar issue: their growth did not necessarily correspond with more money. More services provided does not always equal more profit. As you can imagine, the first thing we did was look into the business model and try to find an area that could be easily adjusted and make a sizable impact.

> More services provided does not always equal more profit.

Medical providers have a standardized coding system that ranks each patient visit on a scale of complexity from one to five. One is the least complex, and five is the most complex. Insurance providers pay medical practices based on that individual code. Since this code affected every single patient visit, we knew that any errors or mistakes here would be dramatically amplified. To revisit the mechanic shop example, this would be comparable to bringing a vehicle into the shop—something necessary for every single transaction. So, we found our variable, frequent cost, and another clear example of an operational lever.

As we examined the rate of coding errors, we found out that the doctors at that practice actually did *more* than they coded. For example, a doctor might code a visit as a level two, when in reality, the complexity should have made it a level four. Once again, we see that the key here is that the action is repeated frequently and therefore multiplied a lot. We found the opportunity to make small changes that would have a big financial impact.

In this situation, there was a discrepancy between the work actually done, and the work billed. Our next job was to find out what could cause the discrepancy. Coincidentally, this also came down to training. The providers at this practice had not been trained to code. They were left to fend for themselves in this area, and they drastically underestimated what code they needed to input. This error, multiplied by several visits per day, cost the practice millions of dollars.

Notice that in both of these examples, the issue was not a staffing redundancy or a technical problem. Operational levers frequently tie into how people evaluate their own work. In nine out of 10 businesses, at least one operational lever will be related to how people are able to track and evaluate their progress on a job. A key point to make here is that operational levers deal with people. For many businesses, payroll is the highest cost. Naturally, many companies—especially service businesses—have operational levers in areas that are directly tied to people.

Operational levers and your projects

Growing pains can result in lost money when it comes to operational levers. As companies get bigger, managers and owners can focus too much on project completion and forget about day-to-day operations that can add up over time. For example, some web development companies bid in the millions to build a large company's website. If they win the bid, they'll assign 20-30 programmers to a project at the same time. If a growing company doesn't know how to manage that many moving parts, the operation won't be tight. I've seen several companies that don't break this type of project down into pieces.

> As companies get bigger, managers and owners can focus too much on project completion and forget about day-to-day operations that can add up over time.

The problem, once again, comes down to employees who don't know how much time it should take to complete a given task. If you have a job that pays a million dollars that should take 200 hours, but it ends up taking 300 hours, you won't find out how much money you'll lose until the very end. It could work the opposite way, too. What if you made more money than expected because you went under on hours?

A lot of companies aren't managing processes or products as well as they should, which makes operations inefficient. My job is to reverse that negative trend for my clients. My advice to this web development company would be to standardize the process in order to make it clear as day to employees how long every task should take. If a programmer is assigned to create one page on any given day, make sure he or she knows if it's expected to take eight or 18 hours. Do you have anyone on staff whose job it is to monitor that? Or, do you just get the job done and cry about lost money later?

Owners stumble when they don't know how long a task should take, either. If you don't have this standardized system in place, it will take some time to create, but make it a priority. The owner of the web development company needs to reach out to a programmer and see how long specific tasks should take. Get everyone on the same page in this area, and don't make employees feel bad for taking longer to deliver a quality product. Instead, take note so you'll know better moving forward.

> **Owners stumble when they don't know how long a task should take.**

I like to see every step of a project broken down, no matter how big the project or small the task. What's the job? How many hours should it take? Empower your employees to speak up when something can't be done within the estimated timeframe. They should be comfortable saying, "no, this can't be done." Maybe the problem is that the employee doesn't understand the task, or maybe whoever assigned the task didn't understand how long it would take. What you should take away from this is that money is made or lost by workers on the shop floor. If nobody on your team knows that the amount of hours listed on a bid isn't manageable, then there is absolutely nothing to do about it but lose money at the end of a project. If we catch it early, though, there is a problem that can be solved.

This type of issue impacts every company of every size, no matter the product or service. At a body shop, every mechanic should have an idea of how long a job will take. If they don't, a supervisor certainly should. It's a huge problem, and a common problem for supervisors not to know, either. As an owner, that would be the time to manage the operation, so you don't have to just wait and hope for the best. Set up an early warning system to see if there are problems so you can solve them before wasting time, money, and materials on something that's not in line with what the company anticipated.

I've worked with overwhelmed owners who push back at this stage. They usually move into action, though, when they realize how much additional profit there is to be made if they fix those issues. It is worth the time to break down every project and measure its effectiveness, no matter if it's a florist creating a bouquet or a contractor making something for the military. Efficiency is important. It's not about beating people on the back yelling at them to go faster, though, but about becoming more effective as you move along. There is a lot of wasted profit flushed down the

> Set up an early warning system to see if there are problems so you can solve them before wasting time, money, and materials on something that's not in line with what the company anticipated.

toilet by owners with great intentions but a lack of systems in place to warn them soon enough to catch a problem. If you're on a ship, you want to be warned about an iceberg when it is miles away, not yards. You don't, and you can't fix everything right away, but you can right the course.

Another common operational lever I help clients find relates to invoicing and collection. If you find yourself with an abnormally high percentage of overdue payments, you will find that you can make significant progress with a few changes. Every business deals with overdue payments. Think about it this way: if you have a payment that you've been waiting on for three months, then you are giving your client a three-month, interest-free loan. Can you really afford to do that? Probably not.

Operational levers and company culture

Even owners who are reluctant to change typically know when there is a problem. They just don't have a feel for how to fix it anymore. They don't know the process because they don't take the time to look at individual jobs or products. Sometimes when an owner is still making money, they don't realize there is more to be made.

Businesses are full of problems. In fact, if there weren't problems, there would not be a need for any businesses. You just need to figure out what's in front of you that can be fixed. The next step is to make sure you have a culture that supports the change.

A company's culture might say, "don't change that," even if there is a system in place. That's why you must encourage employees to throw up a red flag. It's better to fix a problem in real-time than to sweep it under the rug. If you have employees who have learned to put their heads down and ignore efficiency problems, then a cultural shift needs to happen.

Empower employees to have an attitude of problem-solving.

You may notice there is a problem, but it takes the people on the front lines to fix it. Floor managers are crucial here, but it's the front-line workers who have to want to make the changes. Empower them to have an attitude of problem-solving. Train your employees on specifics of the job, so if something goes wrong, they know how to fix it. Great companies hold meetings of the minds right there on the front lines. The decisions made on the floor are worth millions in lost profit or additional profit. Sometimes you just have to look for it if your company is already profitable and not in trouble.

A side benefit to making these changes is that it makes your company a more enjoyable place to work. Companies spend most of their money on operations, which is where there is the most opportunity for increased efficiency. It's common to see companies that have a $10 million payroll in operations and a $3 million payroll in accounting. In most of those businesses, owners are more likely to dig into the accounting department's inefficiencies than operations. I encourage my clients to look into operations to see where people can be more effective, in turn saving money. A lot of owners want to go back and start counting pencils again when we talk about improving profits. It's a silly example, but if your pencil budget is $400 per year, there is no sense in having an *extra* person watch *every* pencil. Get involved with an operational lever that can pay off and have the biggest benefit.

Everything we've covered so far on operational levers spells out a win-win situation for the owner and the employees. If money is lost, there will be hell to pay. Jobs will be lost, and there will be nothing anybody can do about it. Catch problems when they are little, don't punish employees for them, and don't look the other way when your warning systems catch a discrepancy.

Your company's operational levers

At this point, you're probably wondering how to identify some of these inflection points in your own business. While it may be helpful to talk to a professional, such as a coach or consultant, because they give you an unbiased third-party perspective, there are things you can begin to look at to get a sense of what might be affecting your business the most. Following the steps I'm about to list will allow you to take a high-level look at what operational levers might exist in your business.

1. Look in the revenue function

SALES

As chapter five covered in detail, there has to be a sales process in place. There are a lot of CRM software options available to help you automate large parts of the sales process. This frees up your sales team's time, helping them to better serve potential and existing customers. If you can reduce the time it takes to gain a customer, you reduce the cost.

MARKETING

So often, businesses do not have a real marketing plan, which is problematic. If you're not analyzing how your marketing is performing, then it is likely that you are wasting money.

SALES MANAGEMENT

Again, this deals with the ground we covered in chapter five when we discussed sales managers. If there is no sales process, there is a lot of wheel-spinning and not much traction.

2. Product manufacturing process

BE THE EXPERT

The key to finding operational levers in the manufacturing process is to know your sub-process extremely well.

TECHNOLOGY

The right technology can speed up the process. Identifying anything that can make this process more efficient can be a game-changer.

REDUCING WASTE

It doesn't just save the planet, it saves you money. Waste management is a major aspect of the manufacturing process, and therefore a potential operational lever. Getting rid of byproducts costs money, and this is a process that gets repeated.

SHIPPING AND STORING

This is another part of the process where you need to be an expert. These areas produce substantial ongoing costs that frequently get overlooked. Is there a more efficient way to call up an item when it needs to be shipped?

MATERIALS AND PARTS

You guessed it, these are items that are used repeatedly. They directly affect every single transaction.

3. Payroll

THINK EFFICIENCY

This is where most of your money is likely spent, which is why I often receive pushback when I bring this area up to owners. Drastic staffing reductions are rarely the best option, especially for smaller businesses. Remember, operational levers are not about cutting costs but increasing efficiency.

JOB DESCRIPTIONS

A slim minority of businesses actually create and maintain accurate job descriptions. In smaller companies, an employee may have a catch-all role to pick up slack that really isn't in their job description. Responsibilities shift constantly, which makes keeping job descriptions up to date rather difficult. However, this is also where many companies see a lot of waste, whether from an individual doing a job he or she isn't qualified to perform (and the necessary time for another team member to redo the work), from duplicate work, or from people taking time away from their other responsibilities to handle crisis issues.

ORGANIZATION CHARTS

Some kind of chain of command is necessary. Whether you want to build the formal hierarchy into the culture of your organization using job titles, or if you want to enjoy the benefits of a flatter structure, an organization chart is necessary. As we just mentioned, job descriptions get tested in crisis situations. Your organization chart can serve as a built-in backup plan that takes one step out of the response process. However, organization charts are also valuable when you're not in crisis mode. If you've been following along with the steps in this book, then I hope you're experiencing fewer of those crazy days. On a regular day, the organization chart has the same benefits: it streamlines the delegation and reporting process. When everyone knows who they report to and who reports to them, you get CC'd on fewer emails. That alone is worth a lot!

REENGINEERING

Owners need to be open to the possibility of reengineering. There are technical advances that may be useful for your business. It is important not only to keep abreast of the changes in the industry technology you use but to also look for new technologies that can streamline your processes. Regularly updating your processes also encourages innovation within your organization.

GET MORE OUT OF PAYROLL

$1 in payroll = $2-3 in gross revenue, which might quadruple your profit.

TAKE A STEP BACK

There are a lot of numbers and technical information here. Let's simplify this as much as possible. What are things that happen in your business on a daily or weekly basis? Are there recurring tasks that touch multiple people or require more than one person to complete? These areas are ripe for change.

Stay the course

User error is a factor in every single aspect of your business. Each area varies in its potential for user error, though. For example, manual data entry has an extremely high potential for user error. Manufacturing machine processes have a low potential for user error. Communicating with clients is somewhere in the middle. You get the idea.

The idea of operational levers is closely related to your employees and contractors. Any changes in the process will affect them and their work. Implementing changes (which is at the heart of operational levers) can be difficult work. In order to get buy-in from stakeholders, you have to sell them on the idea. Sometimes you have to start with yourself, though.

1. Sell yourself on the idea

MOTIVATE YOURSELF

Before you bring this to your team, it is important that you are committed to the changes you are making. You are the first person you need to sell on these concepts. So how do you motivate yourself to make these necessary changes?

CALCULATE THE IMPACT ON PROFIT

The most compelling argument you can make is to sit down and create a real estimate for how this could affect your company's financials.

IMPACT ON YOUR LIFE

With more profit for less hassle, you are freeing up your time and energy to continue working on the business. You will have more time to spend on your personal life and to create peace.

2. Sell others

CULTURAL CHANGE TAKES TIME

Be realistic about your timeframe. As an owner, it is always tempting to get frantic about what you want to achieve. All you can focus on is how much time you have already wasted. Everything seems like it needed to be done yesterday. However, not everyone will share this urgency. There is validity to this perspective. The people within your organization see things from the tactical level and may have a better perspective on how long it will really take to get things up and running. In order to inspire and motivate your staff, it is necessary to understand the perspective of the group you are encouraging to change. While you have been ruminating about this change for some time, your team has not been focused on the same things. You might want the new system to be implemented by the end of the day, but that probably is not feasible.

It will take a conscious effort on your part to maintain progress made. The natural tendency for people is to revert to long-term behaviors. Making changes was not easy.

When unexpected problems relating to the change spring up, it is tempting to completely abandon the changes. However, by expecting the unexpected issues to arise, it is possible to deter knee-jerk reactions and stay the course. You also need to be wary of issues arising that are unrelated to the change because they can trigger long-term behavior, as well. During a crisis, people often turn to autopilot behaviors on unrelated tasks, enabling them to devote full energy to the crisis.

It will take a conscious effort on your part to **MAINTAIN PROGRESS MADE**.

The natural tendency for people is to revert to long-term behaviors.

CHAPTER 7
Money

OVER THE PAST 30-PLUS YEARS working as a CPA, my team and I have consulted with more than 1,300 businesses. We refer to the money problems we see business owners face over and over again as the Nasty Nine Owner Issues. Some of the issues in this chapter are summarized from previous chapters, but they are common pitfalls worth reviewing. You don't want to fall victim to any of the Nasty Nine, but chances are you already experience a couple of them. The good news is that when you're aware of them, you can prevent them.

1. A mindset problem with understanding profit

Business owners kid themselves sometimes when they talk about how much profit they're making. The problem is that they often do not measure real profit, and sometimes they don't even pay themselves. In reality, a company is not making any profit until the owners get paid fair market value. You need to consider the value of your own labor because you may be underestimating how much you're actually working. I've worked with so many clients who have done this that it made me realize it is a mindset problem in how owners look at profitability.

It's common for owners of smaller businesses not to take a salary for themselves. Yet, they still report that they made a profit. If an owner told me his company's bottom line was $100,000 for the year, but he didn't pay himself, I would argue that the business made no profit because that figure represents the value of the owner's labor. How much could that owner make if he went to work for another company? The profit reported by a small business should be over and above the fair market value of the owner's salary. I would recommend that the owner in this example pay himself a $100,000 salary and correctly show that the company showed zero profits.

What's the point of owning your own business if you are shorting yourself on what you could be making elsewhere? I have a client who is a cardiologist and started his own practice. The year he came to me, his company made

$300,000, and he drew a salary of $100,000. He wasn't struggling by any means, but he could easily get $500,000 a year working for someone else. When you do the math, the value of his labor was $400,000 more than he actually paid himself. Now, if we look at the $300,000 he reported the business made and subtract the $400,000, his company didn't make $300,000. It lost $100,000.

This is the mindset problem with profitability. Sometimes owners pay themselves nothing. Sometimes they pay themselves more than the value of their labor, but they are rarely right on this number. When you're going to analyze how your business is doing, you have to make some adjustments to your books and records. Did you really make money? If so, how much? Almost all companies face this issue, and very few make adjustments to fix it.

2. Out-of-control jobs and overruns

Out of control jobs and overruns are as significant as profit leak. Depending on the type of business, out of control jobs are common. For many business owners, their number one expense, or investment, is payroll.

Recently, I was coaching a client who does environmental work. His company started work on a $1.3 million contract, and everything looked great. When all was said and done, though, it broke badly for him. Based on the proposal he put together, he expected to make 20-30 percent on the job. As it turned out, he lost $200,000.

That might sound absurd to you, but I guarantee that at least 50 percent of businesses have similar problems due to poor management. I tell my clients that if they want to do better, they have to put systems in place. If something is supposed to take six hours, certainly it can't take 10, right? This is where the problem exists, though. When this type of overrun happens day in and day out, it can add up to a multi-million dollar problem.

Out of control jobs and overruns are where money is lost, and my team consistently finds that most owners don't look for these problems. Instead, they waste time on trivial tasks that make little difference, such as micromanaging costs for office supplies. Owners need to focus on the big items, not the trivial. Go where the dollars are, and that's where you can save profits.

Owners need to focus on the big items, not the trivial.

Whether you're in the business of repairing cars, building websites, or consulting, the issue comes back to project management of the different services and projects you produce. When I talk about this, clients tend to think they need to buy new software to track manufacturing. That's not what I'm talking about. You have to empower the workers on the front line, and you need an early warning system.

When we discussed operational levers in chapter six, we covered how the employee doing the job needs to know how long it will take. If they are assigned a job that should be done in eight hours, and they think that's impossible, there is a bigger issue. Either they don't know what the job requires (and need to have that discussion with a supervisor), or a change order needs to be discussed with the customer. This is one of the only stages in a project where action can be taken against overruns. I would rather an employee not start a job if they don't think it can be done in the time allotted.

If a construction company bids $500,000 to build a house, they have to be able to manage progress on a daily basis so nothing goes wrong. Let's say there is an issue installing the custom fireplace cover ordered by the customer. The crew should stop and ask the customer how they should proceed. Let them decide if you should send it back or charge them more money to fix it. If you hold onto that issue until the end of the project, either you're going to lose money or have an unhappy customer. Everyone involved benefits from the client knowing about the problem early.

I experienced a similar problem from a customer's point of view once when I took my car to the shop before a long road trip with my family. I asked the mechanic to make sure my three-year-old car would be ready for the drive. After I dropped off the vehicle, my expectation was the mechanic would inspect it and call me to with his recommendations.

I anticipated needing new tires, an oil change, a realignment, new brake pads, etc. Instead of asking permission to make the repairs, they went ahead with the work and didn't communicate anything with me. At the end of the day, I got a call saying the car was ready and that

I owed thousands of dollars. I was not happy, as you can imagine. My car may very well have needed all of the repairs that they made, and I probably would have signed off on them, but I did not appreciate that they took the decision process away from me. They did a fine job with the repairs, and my car did not break down on our trip, but they lost me as a customer due to the lack of communication.

This story illustrates the importance of dealing with a business issue as soon as something goes awry. If an employee puts his or her head down and does the work, which is how it goes down at most companies, that is when you run into huge problems. Once new parts are installed on a job, there is not much else you can do. Most companies have millions in lost profit on just this issue alone.

3. People management

Get the right person, and it will make all the difference.

Paying your employees is the most significant investment you're going to make every year. Consider your worksite or office. How much money are you paying to get a project done? No matter how long a project takes, time and wages add up quickly. You can't just sit back, hope everything goes well, and expect your people do what they're supposed to do.

People management is a vast area that most owners don't pay attention to because they are only looking at the big picture. They lose sense of how much they are paying their people. I get calls about this from clients all the time. A client has a $40 million company and wants to hire a new controller. The salary for this position has been about $100,000 annually. However, there's one candidate who wants $20,000 more. The business owner is having a real problem deciding what he can afford. In fact, he has been fixated on this issue for eight weeks. There are three candidates, two are decent, and one wants $20,000 more than the other. People are your best investment. Get the right person, and don't worry about the nickels and pennies. *Get the right person, and it will make all the difference.* If you waste $100,000 on someone for their salary, plus $50,000 of *your time* training them, and all that goes away, it was a waste. The first thing you have to do is forget about the money. The reality is that if you hire the right person, that extra $20,000 is irrelevant. If you get the wrong person, it's going to cost you a lot more than $20,000.

Issues like these also tie into your Mission, Vision, and Values. Owners often have a real problem with the way they look at people management. There is a ton of money going out the door if you don't have written MVV statements or if your employees don't know them. Think about it like this. If your staff doesn't know what a good day is, how are they going to have one? Your employees have to know your company's "why." They have to know what kind of business you're in.

If your staff doesn't know what a "good day" is...

HOW ARE THEY GOING TO HAVE ONE?

My people know we're in the business of loving people. Of course, some other things go along with it. I'm not sure we've got the perfect situation, but I think it's essential to think about your MVV.

It's all about the people. Think about what you spend on payroll. Think about how much time you spend thinking about payroll. Keep an eye on operations and the efficiency of operations. Stop wasting time looking at other things that don't make a difference.

People management is a big area where owners have problems. People hire the Plack Group to make money. "Make more money, pay less tax, and live life better." That's our deal. So focus on this area if you want to make more money, too.

4. Sales process problems

Sales process problems are a huge issue, too. As business owners, we're always looking at people who want to sell us that magic bullet, right? If we just hire this one guy, this one salesperson, this one sales manager, or buy this marketing program, everything would be better. But mainly we're talking about sales here. We want to have that magic bullet that we can just buy and expect instant results from. Time and time and time again your plan doesn't work, though, because you have the wrong expectations. You still have to manage a salesperson and even a sales manager. Before you do anything, before you even start to manage them, you've got to have some kind of process.

Only a handful of businesses have a written sales process. And that's a big problem. We want to keep throwing money at it without doing the basic blocking and tackling of having some kind of written sales process. We all know we should do it. These are issues that many companies have, and millions of dollars can be recovered by creating a process.

5. Marketing Confusion

When companies try to be all things for all people, it's not good business—it's marketing confusion, and it's way too common. I coach my clients to be consistent with their messages across all media.

I worked with the owner of a cabinetry company who dealt with marketing confusion. Cabinets are diverse products because almost every type of building needs them. Some jobs are relatively simple, such as a home kitchen remodel. Others are larger and more complex, such as installing cabinets for an office, hospital, or entire apartment building.

> When companies try to be all things for all people, it's not good business— it's *marketing confusion*.

My team took a diagnostic approach and looked to see if messaging was consistent across all of the company's materials: websites, brochures, signs, magazine ads, commercials, product literature, location décor, etc. What we found was a pretty typical example of mixed messaging. The website made the company seem like a high-end installer of cabinets for medical facilities, but the showroom was almost entirely home kitchen displays.

I had no problem with the diversity of this company. In fact, the owner was smart to be in different markets. The problem was consistency. You can effectively market different product lines as long as you have marketing material for all of them, from showroom, to website, to social media.

In the area of marketing, you can't afford confusion because you'll just waste money, and chances are you've probably already spent a lot in that area. Many companies experience marketing confusion because they've been around for more than 20 years and have never

> You can't afford confusion because you'll just waste money.

updated all of their material at once. It's common for companies to make a website one year, print magazine ads another, and run the same commercial for ten years. Now they are delivering too many messages to customers.

Other companies run into problems with marketing confusion because the message they *say* conflicts with what they actually *do*. Here are some questions to consider about your company's marketing:

- Do you know who your top competitors are?

- How are they marketing themselves?

- What are your methods?

- What are your messages?

- Do you spend money on professional branding?

Trying to grow a company without solid branding is like hitting yourself in the head with a hammer while you're trying to run. It is self-defeating and confusing to everybody.

6. No tax planning

Taxes are an area most business owners only think about once a year. They go to a CPA at the end of the year with their information. Later, the returns are complete, and they either owe money or get some back. The problem here is that the CPA is a historian and can only tell them what happened in the past. They can't do anything about the last financial year in the present.

Everyone needs tax returns prepared, but I get my clients to be proactive at tax planning all year. We sit down with clients in June. This is because after the end of the year, there is not much they can do to change things. Owners have already spent the money the way they spent it. We talk about it in June when there is still time to minimize what clients owe. Being proactive is key—don't hire a historian to tell you about the past.

Once, we were able to help a client who knew he would soon be buying a building save money on his taxes. Since we knew ahead of time, we advised him to do a cost segregation study. What probably would have been a $50,000 deduction ended up being $400,000. If he dropped all his books on his CPA at the end of the year, nothing could be done, but since we knew enough to complete the study, the deduction was accelerated.

I found out a new client, who owned an extremely profitable company, did not take any compensation for himself. He also didn't take any costs out of the company account except for payroll. It can be tax advantageous to take money out for things such as employee benefits and health savings accounts, but he didn't know any of that since he only had historical tax work done. We went in, made a plan, changed the compensation structure for the owner, and ended up saving him $40,000 that year.

A lot of companies pay as much as 49 percent in taxes. Saving money here is a big deal and increases the net return of the business. You can only be proactive by having someone tuned in and wrapped around your operation. My team's job is to take more than 50,000 pages of tax law and make our clients aware of the 50 pages that can drop money into their pockets.

With new tax laws come changes to the tax method you use, such as cash basis versus accrual. Most growing businesses will pay less tax under the cash method, but prior to 2019, there were restrictions on who could use this method. Those have been relaxed, and business owners should consider the cash method for tax purposes.

7. Personal Net Worth

I cringe when owners tell me they don't have anything in their retirement plan. Many of them tell me that they are investing in their business instead. While this may be true one year, it shouldn't be the case seven years in a row. At some point, your business has got to be healthy enough. You've got to force it to be healthy and be able to have enough cash flow to take what you're worth, including retirement contributions and profits over and above them.

If you're in this situation, you're not thinking about the long-term picture. If you don't put money away for yourself, who else will? You're not working a government job with a pension. We need to think about how profitable our businesses are, but unfortunately, many owners don't think that through and still believe they had a great year.

To save for your future, put a routine in place that is consistent and can eventually run on autopilot. When owners ignore their personal savings and retirement accounts to keep money in the business, they aren't thinking about the importance of their own net worth.

> Think of a retirement plan like a three-legged stool.

I encourage my clients to think of a retirement plan like a three-legged stool. The first leg is the value of the business. Owners bank on that value growing so they can get paid when they sell the company. You can't rely on that, though. The second leg is a personal retirement plan, such as a

401(k) or IRA. These often get ignored by owners betting on the sale of their companies. You absolutely need to invest in portfolios, though. The third leg of the stool is real-estate, either personal or related to the business. If an owner who is 40 years old personally buys the building where his company operates, then by the time he or she retires, they own a piece of commercial property that they can continue to rent out.

Thinking about retirement can be overwhelming, especially if you haven't been planning. If that's you, start by immediately getting into a regular savings plan for retirement and personal emergencies. Open a 401(k) and put away a certain amount every month. Next, make sure you have a personal emergency plan. An owner requires a bigger emergency plan than most people. Work toward saving six months' worth of expenses that you can access at a moment's notice. You may think this is unrealistic, but start putting a certain amount away today, and over time it will build.

Successful business owners don't say "some day," they set up routines that benefit themselves personally. Here are some questions to consider about your net worth and retirement plan:

- Did you max out your retirement plan?

- Were you able to put $50,000 into your retirement plan?

- Do you have your car on the books?

- Should you have a car on the books?

- Are you looking out for yourself *and* the business?

- Are you looking at what is going well?

8. Working too much

Most business owners work too much. This is a lifestyle issue. As I always say, your business will take all the time you plan to give it, plus 20 percent. There will always be more to be done. The owner must constrain his or her hours so they can protect their lives and relationships.

When you're not in the business, you provide opportunities for the team to grow. Over the years we have found that the less the owner works, the healthier the business is. This is counter-intuitive, yet true.

I recently met a couple at a Christmas party and this topic came up. We got talking, and the wife said, "We have got to hire somebody because he's always working. We can't get away for vacation!" The husband added, "Well, it's not that bad." Two weeks later they came to my office as new clients. I asked the husband to walk me through a typical workday. He reported that he gets to the office around 7 a.m. and leaves between 6:30 and 7 p.m. After dinner, he works for another couple of hours on the computer. He also comes in on Saturdays, but never Sundays. All those hours add up, and we find that most people get addicted to that pattern.

Most business owners **work too much.**

This is a lifestyle issue.

The business can do better; the owner can do better. You *do* have options. This routine is not healthy for the owner, his wife, his family, or the company. Everything and everyone would benefit if he gained control, restricted his hours, and managed his time better between the business and his family life.

> One of our most successful strategies is that we get people to work less.

One of our most successful strategies is that we get people to work less. When I say this, clients look at me like I'm absolutely nuts, but the reality of it is that in the end, they become more effective.

I have tested a theory and proven that when you rest and take time off, you refresh your creativity. When you have no bandwidth, there's no creativity. When you're overworked, you go through the motions trying to get everything done, get the product out the door, and get ready to do it all again the next day. However, when you make time and space to think, the amount of creativity that gets freed up is impressive. Personally, I think that's the key to solving any of the Nasty Nine. Creativity fuels solving problems.

9. Doing the wrong work

We do a lot of things—some that we think we're good at, some we think we like, and some we know we don't. We cling to the idea that we can't give these tasks to anyone else, though. It's a sickness. You're never going to build a business that way.

If you do, everything is going to come down to you. You're going to be the bottleneck.

Ask yourself, what are the three most important things you do that *nobody else* can do? My goal is to spend 80 percent of my time on just those three things and find someone else to take what's left. It can be scary sometimes, especially if you've had the business for a long time and have held onto these responsibilities the whole time.

About three or four years ago, I completed a time inventory like you read about in chapter one. I recorded what I was doing every 15 minutes for a week. This exercise made me realize I was spending *40 percent* of my day dealing with email. It had never occurred to me that someone else could help with my inbox problem. I hired someone to streamline my emails by responding to some and organizing others for me to see later. I've had somebody do that for me ever since, and it has freed up a considerable amount of my day that I can now commit to other things. If you would have tried to convince me the day before I started this time inventory that I was wasting almost half my time with emails, I would have never believed you. I would have said, "No, I respond to emails pretty quickly. I use Dragon to dictate them." I would have listed all the reasons that it couldn't be true, but I would have been mistaken.

Conclusion

WE'VE WORKED WITH MANY CLIENTS over the years who have fallen victim to the issues we've discussed in this book. Many of these people think they have everything under control when they start working with me, but most don't. If you're thinking, *these things are interesting, but they aren't my problems,* I can tell you right now that you're probably lying to yourself. I've looked at many companies over the years, and these are widespread issues. When I take on a new client, my job is to get working on the highest-leverage areas. What are the easiest issues we can take care of that will get clients the best value? Typically, that's starting somewhere in the Nasty Nine. If you don't think this is you, I encourage you to take a few minutes and just think through it. If you want to give me a call to talk through it, I'm happy to do that. Contact us to start a conversation. Visit our website at https://plack.com, email us at info@plack.com, or call us at 410-893-9100.

AFTER MORE THAN 30 YEARS in this line of work, I've learned that focusing on the basics makes a big difference. This is true in life, as well. If you're upside down in some of the One-Life Game Plan™ areas we discussed in this book, all it takes is a few clicks to turn things around. You don't need to make a revolutionary change. Usually, just a 20-percent change will give you a much better outcome. What I see with most clients is an evolutionary change. If you make little changes from month to month, then in a couple of years, you will see that not only have you improved your situation, you have also built yourself a brand new life.

Bibliography

Allen, D. (2002). *Getting Things Done: The Art of Stress-Free Productivity* (Reprint ed.). Penguin Books.

Christensen, C. M., Allworth, J., & Dillon, K. (2012). *How Will You Measure Your Life?* Harper Business.

Cloud, H. (2016). *The Power of the Other: The startling effect other people have on you, from the boardroom to the bedroom and beyond-and what to do about it.* Harper Business.

Covey, S. R., Merrill, R. A., & Merrill, R. R. (1996). *First Things First* (Reprint ed.). Free Press.

Cron, I. M., & Stabile, S. (2016). *The Road Back to You: An Enneagram Journey to Self-Discovery.* IVP Books.

Gerber, M. E. (2004). *The E-Myth Revisited: Why Most Small Businesses Don't Work and What to Do About It* (Updated, Subsequent ed.). Harper Business.

Harnish, V. (2014). *Scaling Up: How a Few Companies Make It...and Why the Rest Don't* (Rockefeller Habits 2.0) (1st ed.). Gazelles, Inc.

Harter, B. J. (2020, October 19). Employee Engagement on the Rise in the U.S. Gallup.Com. https://news.gallup.com/poll/241649/employee-engagement-rise.aspx

Inbox Zero. (2007, October 9). [Video]. YouTube. https://www.youtube.com/watch?v=z9UjeTMb3Yk

Kim, C. W., & Mauborgne, R. (2015). *Blue Ocean Strategy, Expanded Edition: How to Create Uncontested Market Space and Make the Competition Irrelevant* (Revised ed.). Harvard Business Review Press.

Lencioni, P. M. (2012). *The Advantage: Why Organizational Health Trumps Everything Else In Business* (J-B Lencioni Series) (1st ed.). Jossey-Bass.

Stanley, A., Jones, L., & Joiner, R. (2004). *Seven Practices of Effective Ministry*. Multnomah.

Sullivan. (2020, June 26). *Premier Business Coach For Entrepreneurs | Strategic Coach*. The Strategic Coach. https://www.strategiccoach.co.uk/

Summerlin. (2006). *ASLA 2006 Student Awards*. Https://www.Asla.Org/Awards/2006/Studentawards/282.Html.

Thoreau, H. D. (2012). *Walden*. Empire Books.

Why Some Men Pretend to Work 80-Hour Weeks. (2017, December 5). Harvard Business Review. https://hbr.org/2015/04/why-some-men-pretend-to-work-80-hour-weeks/

Acknowledgements

THIS BOOK WAS A JOY TO WRITE. It has been percolating in me for ten years. I am thankful for the many people who helped me get this book to where it is today.

First, I want to thank Cathy Plack, my wife, who has encouraged me to write this book for 20 years and has helped me develop all of its ideas, especially over the last decade. Without her, this project would not exist.

I want to thank my daughter, Ashley O'Donnell, who helped put together a draft of this book and set the vision for how to get things out of my brain and down on paper.

Her assistance was absolutely vital in completing this project. At one time it seemed so overwhelming, but after working with her and getting some initial drafts completed, I realized this was something we could bring to fruition.

I love and appreciate the whole team at the Plack Group and how they serve our business owner clients. Many of the ideas in this book are based on their work in the trenches on a day-to-day basis over the last 30 years. I am grateful for the way they challenge me and give our clients a world-class experience.

A big thanks to our book team, including Sean Joseph and Josh Mitchell, who were fundamental in getting this thing over the line. It was a gargantuan effort taking it from early manuscripts to an actual completed book in a very short period of time.

ABOUT THE AUTHOR

Harry J. Plack

CPA/PFS, CVA, CFE, CMC

HARRY J PLACK, MANAGING MEMBER OF PLACK GROUP, is responsible for business and profitability planning, tax reduction strategy, mergers and acquisitions, business valuation, succession planning, and general business consulting.

Currently, he handles consulting engagements for a variety of closely held businesses. These engagements have provided an extensive background in:

- Profit improvement for business owners

- Reducing tax burdens through advanced tax strategies

- Valuation for merger, banking, and estate tax purposes

- Formation of family limited partnerships

- Assisting companies build infrastructure to scale their enterprise

He is the creator of the One-Life Game Plan™, a coaching program for business owners and senior executives. The One-Life Game Plan™ is a proprietary program developed while working with hundreds of owners and executives over nearly 30 years.

He has served on a variety of non profit boards including YMCA, Baltimore County Chamber of Commerce, Beachmont, and FCA Northern Maryland.

A widely published writer, Harry is an authority on a variety of business issues. He has published over 150 articles in journals and business periodicals, and is a syndicated columnist on business matters. His curriculum has been used by colleges and universities in their entrepreneurship programs. Harry has been interviewed extensively on radio, television, and in the print media on both the local and national scene, sharing his expertise on diverse business topics.

He received his bachelors degree in Accounting from the University of Baltimore and earned a masters degree in Management from the Johns Hopkins University.

Harry is a CPA and a member of both the American Institute of Certified Public Accountants and the Maryland Association of Certified Public Accountants. Additional certifications include CVA (Certified Valuation Analyst), PFS (Personal Financial Specialist), CFE (Certified Fraud Examiner) and CMC (Certified Management Consultant).

Make more money.
Pay less tax.
Live life better.

TRANSFORM THE WAY YOU DO BUSINESS & LIVE YOUR LIFE.

Contact us to start a conversation.
Visit our website at https://plack.com,
email us at info@plack.com,
or call us at 410-893-9100

PLACK GROUP
SOLUTIONS FOR SUCCESS

410-893-9100   PLACK.COM

CLAIM YOUR FREE RESOURCE

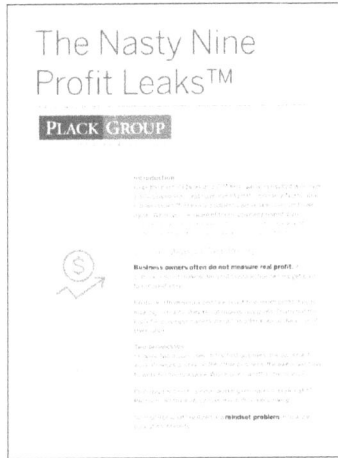

The Nasty Nine
Profit Leaks™

PLACK GROUP

Get the FREE 12-page report and upgrade
your business management! Most business
owners are making BIG mistakes that are easy
to overcome with the help of some powerful
questions. In this exclusive, FREE resource, you
will discover how to better think through…

- How to measure real profit
- Ensure jobs stay in control
- People management strategies
- Sales process upgrade opportunities
- Marketing clarity questions
- Tax planning suggestions
- And much more!

https://plack.com/nastynine/

The One-Life™
Game Plan

Take your next step.
Get freedom. Get control.

As a business owner, you will always have a long to-do list. Our job is to help you determine what is most important and help you move toward your goals each month.

One-Life Game Plan™ coaching services are exclusively designed for the special needs of business owners who want to surge ahead in both their personal and professional life, with both immediate and ongoing results.

If you would like more information, contact us to start a conversation. Visit our website at https://plack.com, email us at info@plack.com, or call us at 410-893-9100.

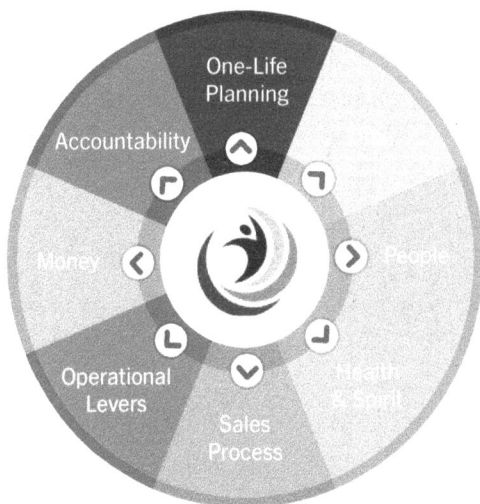

VISIT PLACK.COM/ONELIFE